BUYING BOOKS

A How-To-Do-It Manual for Librarians

Second Edition

Audrey Eaglen

**HOW-TO-DO-IT MANUALS
FOR LIBRARIANS**

NUMBER 99

NEAL-SCHUMAN PUBLISHERS, INC.
New York, London

Published by Neal-Schuman Publishers, Inc.
100 Varick Street
New York, NY 10013

The paper used in this publication meets the minimum requirements of American National Standard for Information Sciences—Permanence of Paper for Printed Library Materials, ANSI Z39.48–1992.

Printed and bound in the United States of America.

Library of Congress Cataloging-in-Publication Data

Eaglen, Audrey.
    Buying books : a how-to-do-it manual for librarians / Audrey Eaglen.—2nd ed.
      p.   cm. — (How-do-do-it manuals for librarians ; no. 99)
    Includes bibliographical references and index.
    ISBN 1-55570-371-2 (alk. paper)
      1. Acquisitions (Libraries) 2. Libraries and publishing. 3. Libraries and booksellers.
    4. Book industries and trade. I. Title. II. How-to-do-it manuals for libraries ; no. 99.

Z689 .E33 2000
025.2'33—dc21

00-041568

For Margaret J. Harris, again, and this time Gail Curley too

CONTENTS

PREFACE

Books are the tools of the librarian's trade. *Buying Books* is a direct result of my conviction that most people who work in libraries know very little about the industry that produces and distributes them. Librarians are frequently frustrated in their attempts to obtain many of the titles vital to the collection building process because of this lack of knowledge. They often fail to understand the unique complexity of the book publishing industry. The librarian, lacking knowledge of the book publishing industry and distribution process, often over-pays for books. The key to better book buying practices is to gain the knowledge, learn the business, and realize how it operates. Libraries are some of the best customers of the publishing industry. I encourage you to use this book as a source of information about and guidance to the book business.

Book publishing is a curious, unique, and paradoxical business. First and foremost, it is a *business*. Publishers must make enough profit to stay in business. They share this common bottom line whether pursuing success in the publishing business for lofty goals or primarily to make profits. Like any other business owner, they must be aware of basic principles of managing a business well enough to assure that profit. Publishers must hire the right people and pay them competitive wages, know the costs of overhead and equipment, and understand the principles of marketing to distribute the product effectively. A book publisher needs all the basic skills an entrepreneur in any other business needs—but there ends the similarity between publishing and most other businesses.

Second, the product in book publishing differs significantly from most other businesses and those differences give rise to its paradoxical nature. A book is a very individual product. If you don't like one brand of aspirin, you can buy any of several other brands; any one will probably relieve your headache. With publishing, each title produced is unique—the result of a singular act of creation by an author, and is not interchangeable with other titles. If you want to read *Jane Eyre*, you will be unlikely to look upon *Vanity Fair* as an acceptable substitute. Books are not interchangeable, and it is the book's very uniqueness that gives rise to a number of problems for librarians. I will discuss these problems in some detail in subsequent chapters.

A third significant factor making publishing different from other businesses stems from the nature of the book. A book is much more than the sum total of the number of words printed on its pages. It communicates an author's ideas; influencing the thinking and ideas of others. This power is rare compared to other manufactured objects—except (although not usually to the same degree as books) magazines, films, videos, and CDs. A book often reflects the culture of a nation, frequently molding or changing that culture. Consider the impact of Rachel Carson's *Silent Spring*, George Orwell's *1984*, or Benjamin Spock's *Baby and Child Care* upon contemporary thought in the United States. And think about the often-monumental efforts to suppress certain books, simply because of this great power to shape ideas, policies, and even actions. This is the paradox of book publishing: part commerce, and yet transcending mere commerce; possibly becoming a powerful cultural force for good or evil. This makes book publishing unique.

Librarians have long recognized the cultural power of the book. Perhaps understanding and respecting the freedom of ideas presented in books initially motivated their career choice to become librarians. Unfortunately, many librarians have paid little attention to the commercial aspects of the book publishing industry. This may have been appropriate in the past. Then only a few thousand titles were published annually and most stayed in print for many years. This was a time when the power of media hype and the enormous buying power of the chain bookstores did not have so great an influence on book publishers and what they publish. It was a time when book wholesaling was a more ethical business than it appears to be today; when the price of books did not escalate at a rate far greater than the price of other goods; and when library budgets were much more stable and predictable.

Many of the factors making book purchasing a veritable pleasure at one time have changed radically over the last three decades. The very nature of book publishing is different. Mergers and acquisitions, the phenomenal growth of bookstore chains, online book retailing, the growing phenomenon of the electronic book, the rise of the "blockbuster" book, the ever-increasing proliferation of new titles each year, the influence of television and movies, and the growing use of Internet are just some of the profound new influences impacting the book publishing industry. At the same time, many other factors have conspired to make the acquisition librarian's lot an unhappy one. These factors include the demise of a number of dependable book wholesaling firms, the astronomical price increase of books, and the perpetuation of publishers' anachronistic distribution processes. These changes have all been set against the backdrop of four decades of overall reduction in library funding. Today's librarian must understand the nature, enormity, and complexities of these changes to effectively develop new collection policies and strategies.

Part One of *Buying Books* offers an extensive and intensive look at book publishing in the United States. Chapter One briefly examines the history of American book publishing and concludes with an overview of the contemporary publishing scene. Chapter Two discusses the major types of book publishing. Chapter Three focuses on the development of a book from author to reader. This first part of *Buying Books* supplies the background information necessary to the librarian who wishes to spend available book funds intelligently given the complex and ever-changing nature of the publishing business. All the issues discussed in the next three chapters have profound effects on a library's collection. The subject of Chapter Four is the distribution process—agreed upon in the book business as the biggest problem facing the industry today. By extension, distribution is also the biggest problem for the librarian trying to purchase books. Chapter Five deals with the increasing expense and the issues of pricing books. Any librarian in a position to buy books should carefully examine Chapter Six, a discussion of current trends in publishing and major influences on the industry.

Part Two builds on background information to help the library book purchaser "do it good"—or at least better. I devote Chapters Seven and Eight to the all-important issue of choosing vendors: the strengths and weaknesses of the various types of wholesalers and distributors, the advantages and disadvantages of buying direct from the publisher or buying from retailers, including those now selling their wares through the Internet. Chapter Nine deals with the ethics of vendor-library relations, and their obligations to one another. Chapter Ten covers the actual process of ordering the book, from pre-order searching and verification to receipt and processing of materials, through the claims and returns processes. Chapter Eleven examines automated acquisitions—looking at the process from making the decision to automate to the various types of software and systems available. This chapter explores various procedures, from independent in-house systems to stand-alone and online systems; and how the availability and economy of personal computers and software can bring a degree of automation, efficiency, and economy in materials acquisitions to even the smallest of libraries at minimal cost. Chapter Twelve discusses the future of the book publishing industry and the possible implications for library book purchasing. *Buying Books* concludes with a glossary of commonly used publishing and acquisitions terms; a selected, annotated bibliography of books and articles for further reading; a list of selected book wholesalers; a list of selected automated acquisitions system vendors; and a subject index.

The nature of the publishing industry will undoubtedly remain volatile. I trust the information learned here will help librarians select books quickly and wisely. It is not overly concerned with the myriad details of the process falling under the broad but vague heading of "acquisitions." This book might be simply described as "how to buy books good." If it succeeds in helping librarians do only that, all the rest of the collection building and acquisitions processes will become a great deal easier, and that in turn will result first in more prudent use of a library's funds and ultimately in better service to all library users.

PART I

THE BOOK
PUBLISHING INDUSTRY:
WHAT IT IS,
WHAT IT DOES

1 BOOK PUBLISHING, PAST AND PRESENT

The book as we know it today is a relatively modern phenomenon in the history of humankind, dating from only about the first century AD, when the first great codex—consisting of flat sheets of parchment bound on one side and protected by a stiff cover of leather—was published. Prior to that, words had been inscribed on a variety of materials and in various forms. The original edition of *Encyclopaedia Britannica*, published in 1771, and itself a landmark in the history of publishing, describes the advent of the book:

> Books were first written on stones, witness the Decalogue given to Moses: Then on the parts of plants, as leaves chiefly of the palm tree; the rind and barks . . . and the Egyptian papyrus. By degrees wax, then leather, were introduced, especially the skins of goats and sheep, of which at length parchment was prepared: Then lead came into use, also linen, silk, horn, and lastly paper itself.
>
> The first books were in the form of blocks and tablets; but as flexible material came to be wrote on, they found it more convenient to make their books in the form of rolls: These were composed of several sheets fastened to each other and rolled upon a stick, or *umbilicus*; the whole making a kind of column, or cylinder, which was to be managed by the umbilicus as a handle, it being reputed a crime to take hold of the roll itself . . . The whole volume, when extended, might make a yard and a half wide, and fifty long.

In spite of its cumbersome size and shape, the roll remained the form of choice for the book over the centuries in ancient Greece and Rome; great libraries like the one at Alexandria, for example, often contained tens, even hundreds, of thousands of volumes.

The advent of the codex changed all this, however, and the roll was soon supplanted by bound sheets, although both the inscribing and binding of these first "modern" books were done by hand, usually in the monasteries of Europe. The next great leap forward in book publishing came some fourteen centuries later with two remarkable developments: the introduction of paper as an inexpensive alternative to parchment and the invention of movable type. Movable type made it possible to print books in volume on a printing press, a method that not only made earlier methods obsolete but also had the effect of making it possible to produce many more books so inexpensively that for the first time the book became accessible to the common people, not just to the nobility and to religious and secular scholars.

During the intellectual ferment of the Reformation and Counter-Reformation, the availability of books became a potent force in disseminating ideas and led to an astonishing rise in the literacy rates of England and Europe. Indeed, when the first settlers arrived in the New World in the early 1660s, the literacy rate in England alone was 60 percent, as compared to 10 percent just a century earlier. It was inevitable that a demand for books would accompany those first settlers to the colonies. In a sense, the American book industry was born when, in 1638, the first printing press arrived in the colonies and was set up in Cambridge, Massachusetts; in 1640 the press printed *The Whole Book of Psalms*, or *Bay Psalm Book* as it is better known—the New World's first best-seller.

Other colonial printers followed suit, although they claimed they could not afford to print anything except that which was paid for in advance, or the work of authors (usually British) whose popularity was great enough to virtually assure that reprints of their books would sell. For instance, Sir Walter Scott's novel *Waverley* sold 8,000 copies on its first day of publication, and the novels of Samuel Richardson and Laurence Sterne often went into several editions. Almanacs were also popular; some of them, notably Nathaniel Ames's *Almanack*, sold 50,000 copies or more each year. But for the most part, the American author who wanted a book published had to assume all costs to have the book printed and distributed; even such popular Americans as Washington Irving followed this practice. Gradually, however, as printers began to accumulate capital, their operations grew, as did their ability to spot a potentially sellable book. It was not long, therefore, before the entrepreneurial spirit overcame caution, and book publishing as we think of it today—as an expansion of the printing business—became an entity in the new American republic.

COLONIAL TIMES TO 1900: THE BEGINNINGS

Mathew Carey was born in Dublin in 1760 and early in his life apprenticed to a printer, where his reading, coupled with his strong political beliefs, led him to attempt writing himself. Resentful of British domination of his beloved Ireland, he penned a series of anti-British pamphlets that soon came to the attention of the British authorities, who threatened him with prison for subversive activities. To escape jail, he fled to France, where he found a job working for Benjamin Franklin and met the Marquis de Lafayette.

In 1784, he left the Continent for good and sailed to America. He soon found work in Philadelphia as a reporter for the *Pennsylvania Herald*. His friendship with Lafayette paid off in 1787, when the marquis offered him money to start his own newspaper, the *American Museum*. The paper was a success from the first and provided Carey with the capital to begin publishing books, the first two of which were American versions of the Roman Catholic and Protestant bibles. Both were highly successful. Encouraged, he decided to branch out into other, more secular, areas of book publishing.

One of Carey's first great successes came in 1793, when he published a novel by a British woman, Susanna H. Rowson. *Charlotte Temple: A Tale of Truth* sold upwards of 50,000 copies. He followed this success by arranging to publish the works of Sir Walter Scott before competitors were able to; before long, Carey was the leading publisher in the United States.

When he retired in 1825, he turned the business over to his son and son-in-law, Henry Carey and Isaak Lea, two gifted and energetic young businessmen who continued to expand the Carey publishing empire. By the late 1820s, the firm was releasing nearly one out of every four books published in the United States. The company survived until the mid-1980s; called Lea & Febiger, it specialized in medical books and journals.

Perhaps inspired by Carey's success, others began to test the book-publishing waters. Joshua B. Lippincott began his career as a book-store clerk in Philadelphia and ended up the store's owner. He soon began publishing religious books and was so successful that a few years later he was able to buy out a major book jobber and expand enormously. By 1853, sales from the store and revenues from his published books reached almost $2 million, an almost inconceivable sum for the time.

Another Philadelphian, Presley Blakiston, began his career working for Carey and Lea. In 1843, he and a friend, Robert Lindsay, decided to try publishing on their own and specialized in books on medicine and science. From the first, Lindsay and Blakiston was successful and became Blakiston Son & Co. when Lindsay retired; eventually it was bought by McGraw-Hill.

But it was in New York that American publishing found its true home. By 1807, when a young man named Charles Wiley opened a bookstore there, New York was already the largest city in the United States and well on its way to becoming the nation's cultural center. Wiley's love of books and ideas led him to offer to help his intellectual writer friends by publishing their books, a practice fraught with risk since there was no guarantee that any of these unknown authors' books would sell. Then Wiley happened to meet James Fenimore Cooper, with whom he reached a publishing agreement; before long enough of these books had sold that Cooper's popularity began to approach that of Sir Walter Scott. Upon Wiley's death at age forty-four, the firm was taken over by his son John, who eventually went into partnership with George Putnam, and Wiley and Putnam became one of America's leading publishers.

In 1848, though, the partnership dissolved. John Wiley concentrated on publishing scientific and technical books; his company, now known as John Wiley & Sons, Inc., remains to this day one of the country's largest publishers of the same kinds of books that the original John Wiley published. Putnam, always more interested in *belles lettres*, went his own way, although he came close to ruin as a result of the pecca-dilloes of a partner who used company funds to indulge in wildcat speculation. Putnam's stint as Collector of Internal Revenue for New York City helped him to bail the company out. As the Putnam Pub-lishing Group, a part of Penguin Putnam Publishing, the company sur-vives and is a major publisher of both adult and children's books.

But it was the four Harper brothers of New York who left the most lasting mark on nineteenth-century publishing. Their rapid expansion and willingness to innovate, coupled with an amazing quality of en-trepreneurial daring, led to Harper & Brothers' position as the largest publisher in the world by mid-century.

Like most of their contemporaries, the Harpers entered the world of publishing as printers. But within a year of opening their print shop in 1817, they had published their first two books, which they mar-keted ingeniously and which sold quite well. Soon they began to pub-lish "serious" books, most of which were religious in nature—in keeping with their Methodist upbringing. Pious, thrifty, hard-work-ing entrepreneurs all, the brothers soon surpassed their arch-rival Mathew Carey in both number of titles published and in profits. A disastrous fire wiped out their extensive plant in 1853, but, undaunted, the Harpers resumed production within a few days.

Even the deaths of the four brothers from 1869 to 1877 did not slow the company down, as all had sons who took over and applied the same talent and dedication to the business that their fathers had. By the 1880s, Harper & Brothers was doing an extremely high vol-ume of business for a publishing house of that era—some $4 million per year. At the same time, the Harpers had a powerful influence on the quality of publishing. By the turn of the century, their roster of authors included such luminaries as Willkie Collins, George Eliot, Henry James, Thomas Hardy, and Mark Twain. Their books ranged from popular fiction through scholarly history to authoritative texts in science and medicine and, although the company would later face a traumatic financial reorganization, it managed to survive and still exists today as the respected firm HarperCollins.

A number of others entered the field during the nineteenth century, many of which are leaders and whose company names remain familiar to readers and librarians to this day. Some of theses are G. and C. Merriam Company (1832); J. B. Lippincott (1836); Little Brown and Company (1837); Bobbs-Merrill (1838); A. S. Barnes (1845); Charles Scribner (1846); David Van Nostrand (1848); E. P. Dutton (1852); Rand McNally (1868); Cornell University Press (the first university press in the United States, 1869); R. R. Bowker (1872); Henry Holt and Company (1873); T. Y. Crowell (1876); Funk & Wagnalls (1878); Houghton-Mifflin (1882); Silver, Burdett and Company (1885); W. B. Saunders Company (1888); The Grolier Society (1895); Doubleday, McClure and Company (1897); McGraw Publishing Company (1899).

In 1900, the American Publishers Association (later to become the Association of American Publishers) was established, with Charles Scribner as its first president. As John Tebbel, in his monumental *A History of Book Publishing in the United States*, puts it, this was a period "when the general organization of the industry was established and the problems which still beset it were defined."

1900 TO 1940: GOING COMMERCIAL

The years from 1900 to 1940 can be characterized as an era of commercialization—when many lasting (and some not-so-lasting) partnerships were formed, when more new publishing houses were established, when houses merged and unmerged, and when the very nature of the publishing business changed radically. The long tradition of father-to-son-to-grandson succession as owners and managers of the powerful publishing houses established before 1900 began to decline, and the forces of finance capitalism started to come to the fore, as when the Harper family firm was reorganized by financier J. P. Morgan in 1899.

No small reason for the weakening of the family ownership tradition was the attitude of publishers themselves toward their business. Earlier printer-publishers had been businesspeople first and "publishers" second, but gradually a transformation occurred to the philosophy that publishing was somehow a cut above other businesses. As Henry Holt maintained to his dying day, it was not a "business" at all, but a "profession."

Holt, as a matter of fact, was one of the first major publishers who did not start his career in the printing industry. Rather, he wanted to be a writer, studied law but never practiced it, and finally entered into business with a young Philadelphia publisher. In short, Holt was a gentleman in what he considered a gentlemanly profession, and he quickly became disillusioned by some of the crasser aspects of business, which never failed to offend his sensibilities. In 1905 the *Atlantic Monthly* carried a long article in which Holt decried what he called "the commercialization of literature" and, speaking of himself no doubt, exhorted his readers to remember that "a few publishers exercise an appreciation of literature in large superiority to financial considerations." In another article published some months later he decried the "accidents [which had] within the past few years so far removed the publishing business from the control of publishers into that of financiers."

By the turn of the century, however, several economic panics, the threat of war with Spain, a series of costly printers' strikes, serious competition among publishers for potential "best-selling" authors, and increases in the cost of doing business—coupled with publishers' own failure to adopt modern business practices—all opened the way for the financiers. Banks and investment trusts that supplied publishers with capital insisted on greater efficiency in the interest of larger and surer profits. The era of "genteel publishing" had ended, and for better or worse, the American book-publishing world would never be the same.

1940 TO THE PRESENT: YEARS OF TURMOIL

[Prior to World War II, the book industry] suffered from a paucity of business acumen.... When an endeavor, by its very nature, attracts people who find their rewards in its nonmaterial aspects, it is not normally going to find the best talent in American business management flocking to its doors. Nor is it likely that the people whom it does attract will arrive with the persuasion that sound management ability is one of the prime requisites expected of them. Thus, many publishing houses become victims of a vicious circle: because they were not successful businesses, they did not enlist the interest of good business people—with the result that they remained largely unsound from a business standpoint.
—John P. Dessauer, *Book Publishing: What It Is, What It Does*

The book industry before World War II was in trouble: sales were low, markets were limited as booksellers struggled to survive, and the Great Depression had, as Dessauer puts it in the book cited above, "intensified what was then, even more than now, a minority interest in books." As a result, the book industry remained a minor segment of American business and was not looked upon favorably by investors with capital to invest.

World War II changed all this in several ways. Older readers and history buffs may recall the ubiquitous slogan, "Lucky Green has gone to war," referring to the fact that Lucky Strike cigarettes, long recognized by their distinctive green package, changed to a white pack to save certain ingredients in the green ink for the war effort. Books, too, went to war; millions of copies of inexpensively bound "Armed Forces Editions" were distributed at no cost to members of the armed forces all over the world, creating a huge new pool of readers (and eventually buyers) of books. On the home front, wartime austerities kept people at home, where books (and the radio) became a primary source of inexpensive entertainment, especially in the new twenty-five-cent paperbound format introduced during this period.

When the war ended, thousands of GIs returned to peace and a virtually free college education, giving college and university textbook sales a huge boost. Many of these same GIs married and settled down, creating the "baby boom" of the 1950s, which in a few years gave rise to a vast increase in the elementary/secondary school populations, thus boosting the sales of textbooks in this area as well.

Business being what it is, it was not long before investment counselors started to take notice of the once nearly moribund publishing industry and began to encourage their clients to invest capital in this "new" growth industry. Both individuals and corporations—some outside the book industry entirely—began to infuse capital into the business while, in other cases, publishers themselves began to initiate mergers with and acquisitions of other publishing companies. As a result, the book-publishing industry began to grow from the cottage industry it had been at the beginning of World War II to a more than $26 billion a year business by 1999.

A look at the number of titles published from 1945 to 1999 indicates the magnitude of that growth better than anything else could. From a total of slightly more than 11,000 titles published in 1941 (and even fewer than that published during the rest of the war years because of paper shortages and other factors), by 1999 the industry was releasing more than 60,000 new titles annually and gave every indication of matching or even increasing that figure well into the millennium. Whatever the feelings about this new era of acquisitions and mergers on the part of those in publishing, there is no doubt that the infusion of new capital into the book industry resulted in spectacular growth for this once-threatened business.

THE CURRENT SCENE

While it is true that the publishing industry at the beginning of the twenty-first century is a far cry from what it was a few decades ago in terms of number of titles published as well as dollar volume, changes in the very nature of publishing and book distribution have been every bit as spectacular—and perhaps more profoundly influential on book-publishing's future—as dollar gains.

Many feared that the large number of mergers and takeovers over the last fifty years would result in a decrease in the number of titles published so that only the most profitable titles, regardless of a book's innate worth, would see the light of day. People also worried that runaway consolidation of publishing houses would lead to only a few of the biggest and most powerful surviving. There is little doubt that certain publishers did feel some corporate pressure to improve the "bottom line" by publishing guaranteed best-sellers at the expense of midlist titles, and that some houses did become giants as a result of the merger trend, so these fears were by and large well-founded.

Rather than decreasing, however, the number of titles published annually increased fivefold. In 1955, 12,000 new titles were published; by 1999, more than 60,000 appeared in *Books in Print*. In 1955, about 110,000 titles were in print; forty-four years later *Books in Print* listed more than 1.9 million. And although some publishers did concentrate their efforts during this period on producing "blockbusters" (as will be discussed in Chapter 6), this phenomenon remained confined to a narrow range of trade publishers. Meanwhile, not only have the numbers of publishers increased tremendously, but publishing has also begun to take on a regional nature it never had. The industry is no longer confined to New York, Boston, and a few other major cities (Chicago and Philadelphia primarily), but has spread to all regions of the country, as was evidenced a few years ago when Harcourt, Brace Jovanovich decentralized much of its New York operation to Cleveland, Ohio, and Orlando, Florida; HarperCollins has long maintained a major operation in San Francisco. In short, the book business has not only made impressive gains in size since 1940 but has also become a national phenomenon.

The spectacular growth of the mass-market paperback business, and its equally rapid decline over the two decades before 1998 (although this segment of the industry showed a substantial increase in late 1998 and 1999), had a great impact on the industry as a whole. While other book categories such as hardcovers and trade paperbacks showed increases in sales during those years, the drop in mass-market paperback sales was approximately 25 percent. Three principal factors account for this:

1. the ruinous rate of returns: more paperbacks are returned to the publisher by bookstores and wholesalers than are sold, with some distributors returning as much as 70 percent of shipments
2. price: a paperback reprint at $8, $9, or $10 (now-common prices) is not that attractive when the $27 hardcover is being discounted at 30 percent or more
3. the increasing trend for mass-market paperback publishers to publish in hardcover; this means that those mass-market paperback publishers who choose *not* to publish in hardcover simply cannot obtain reprint rights to many best-sellers.

Bantam Books, once a publisher of paperbacks only, began to publish in hardcover in the early 1980s and had a string of hardcover best-sellers led by *Iacocca* and *Yeager*; Bantam of course retained paperback rights to these and their other best-selling hardcover titles, and other paperback publishers followed suit. In the mid-1980s, the president of Warner Books referred to the paperback industry as "a very nervous one," and his words held true for more than a decade.

Another factor that has affected the book-publishing industry is the growth of the chain bookstores. Some idea of this growth can be seen in this accounting:

A little more than ten years ago (1970) the four major chains [at that time, Waldenbooks, B. Dalton Booksellers, Crown Books, and Barnes & Noble] sold just under 12 percent of all the trade books published in the United States; by 1980 that figure had tripled. In 1984 just the *two* largest chains [Waldenbooks and B. Dalton Booksellers] [sold] more than half of the trade and mass market books published in this country. (Audrey Eaglen, "Chain Bookstores and Library Collection Building," *Collection Building*, Spring 1984, Vol. 6, no. 1, pp. 24–26)

The chain bookstores depend on huge volume and high profit levels for their success, and they achieve these goals by patterning their operations after those in food supermarkets:

It's no accident that the chain stores are almost always located in or very close to a suburban shopping mall with its supermarkets, discount stores, and shops, and even look like small supermarkets, with point-of-purchase displays near the cash registers . . . bright lighting; colorful signage; carefully calculated loss-leader displays; only a few staff, who usually are young and cut from an entirely different mold than the traditionally knowledgeable and helpful independent bookseller; and scientifically designed walk and display patterns that enable you to browse (but not too long—aisles are narrow as a rule) while directing your browsing toward those items which are normally known as "impulse" items. . . . All this is, of course, predicated on one vitally important element, a "product" that will sell and sell fast; high volume and high turnover is the name of the game. Accordingly, the titles chosen to be stocked by the chains will of necessity consist largely of those titles that are practically guaranteed to sell quickly and well: fad books, best-selling authors' books, easy reference books, recreational books such as puzzle and joke books, bargain "cheap" books (remainders), mass market children's books . . . most of which will be paperback. . . . In short, whatever books, for whatever reason, have had enough "media hype" or have enough intrinsic appeal to the lowest-common-denominator reader, will be stocked, and whatever shows up on the chains' sophisticated computer inventory reports as a "hot," i.e., fast-selling, item will be restocked, again and again if necessary, until its "item velocity" has slowed down enough to warrant its being dropped from inventory and shipped back to its publisher. (*Ibid.*, p. 25)

The lesson should be clear: if publishers are to survive and make a profit, they must consider the potential market that the chain bookstores represent when making decisions about what to publish and what not to publish. It is not unreasonable to assume that publishers will attempt to publish as much as possible that will sell to this market, nor is it unreasonable to predict that, given "bottom-line" pressures, many publishers will consider the chains' needs the standards by which they decide what to publish. If this happens, librarians' options for purchasing books *of all kinds* to build strong collections will become increasingly limited.

Interestingly enough, the situation seems to be just the reverse among wholesalers, even though they too are a very large market for publishers' wares. The two largest wholesalers are Baker & Taylor, which traditionally has sold primarily to libraries, and Ingram Books, which began as a wholesaler to the retail book trade but has increasingly wooed the library market in recent years. Whether or not this serves as a counter-influence to the chains' impact on publishers remains to be seen.

A final major influence on contemporary publishing is what Thomas Whiteside has termed "the blockbuster complex" in his book of the same name—that is, the tendency to publish titles that may become enormous best-sellers at the expense of other books. A few decades ago, mass-market paperback publishers were the worst offenders; just one book, Judith Krantz's *Princess Daisy*, brought $3.2 million from Bantam for paperback reprint rights; with a cover price of $3.95, it is hard to believe that Bantam ever sold enough millions of paperback copies to earn that sum back. Another paperback publishing company, Pocket Books, bought the rights to reprint John Irving's *The Hotel New Hampshire* for a similar sum and later revealed that it lost a million dollars on the deal.

By the mid-1980s, however, many hardcover publishers had also become obsessed with blockbusters. James Michener's *Texas* was a groundbreaking book in that it had a first printing of 750,000 copies and was also the first pop fiction title to break the $20 price barrier; both those factors probably contributed to sales that were described as "disappointing." Michener's book was eclipsed by Crown's first printing of Jean Auel's *The Mammoth Hunters*, whose run was one million copies—at that time the biggest first printing of a hardcover book in the history of publishing. Within a few months of its publication date, *Mammoth Hunters* was listed in several book-remainder catalogs. And the gambling on potential blockbusters continues to this day. In 1998, Warner Books published *Belladonna*, a novel by Karen Moline for which the publisher had paid a $1 million advance; the book sold only about 25,000 copies, several hundred thousand less than the publisher had projected. And even big name authors are not immune to disappointing their publishers. Gary Larson, a proven million-copy seller with his collections of *Far Side* cartoons, couldn't manage to sell even a third of the million copy printing of his 1998 opus, *There's a Hair in My Dirt*, by mid-1999. Even a book by a sitting president was not immune; according to *Publishers Weekly*, President Clinton's *Between Hope and History* "sold only a quarter of its 400,000-plus printing—sales made possible only through additional discounting and promotion." (Readers who would like to read more about the blockbuster follies can find accounts of publishers' more notable flops in *Publishers Weekly*, usually in a spring issue.)

The problems with this concentration on potential blockbusters are obvious. The publication of hundreds of thousands or a million copies of a book requires a major outlay of capital; if such capital is obtained at the expense of publishing books of great import and literary value, then its impact on libraries, which buy both the blockbusters and the books that may sell only a few thousand copies, is negative indeed. At the same time—as many, many publishers have discovered—there is no guarantee of a return on a huge outlay; just a few bad decisions of this magnitude could be and have been the ruination of many publishing houses.

Regardless of the negative effects of many current trends, at the turn of the twenty-first century publishing remains basically a healthy, growing industry that produces an enormous variety of materials for every taste and that can turn a handsome profit for the entrepreneur willing to take risks. As an industry, it is small compared to others; many individual companies of conglomerates generate more volume than all of book publishing's more than $26 billion annually; for example, Exxon had earnings alone of $8.46 billion in 1997 and assets of $96.1 billion. Yet, in terms of influence and importance, probably no other business in the United States can approach the book industry. For libraries, it is undisputedly the most important industry of all.

2 TYPES OF BOOK PUBLISHING

Books are categorized according to three broad factors: the nature of their producers (publishers) and the types of materials they specialize in; the books' intended audience or market; or the method of their distribution to that audience. An example of the first is a university-press book, which is published by a press sponsored by a university and usually intended for a well-educated or scholarly audience. A book published for student use in the classroom at any level from elementary school through undergraduate and graduate schools is generally classified as a textbook and exemplifies the second category. An example of a book categorized primarily by method of distribution is a mass-market paperback; in this case, while the book is probably intended for a large or "mass" audience, the term "mass-market" refers not to the book's intended audience but to its chief method of distribution, which will be discussed later.

The Association of American Publishers (AAP) generally divides published books into ten broad categories for its various studies and reports. These are

1. Trade
2. Religious
3. Professional
4. Mass-market paperbacks
5. University press
6. Elementary and secondary textbooks
7. College textbooks
8. Subscription reference books
9. Mail-order publications
10. Book clubs

Such divisions may be useful for the AAP, but they leave out a number of other kinds of books and publishing such as alternative/small/independent publishing; vanity publishing; reprinting (usually of out-of-print titles) and its contemporary and growing counterpart, thanks to modern technology, of on-demand printing; large-print publishing; publications produced by societies and associations; government publications; audio books and books on CD-ROM; and the most recent phenomenon, e-books—all of which are likely to be purchased by libraries at one time or another. In fact, none of these categories is ever so clear cut; differences among the various kinds of publishing can be more than a little blurry at times. A brief description of the ten AAP categories and those not included by AAP follows.

TRADE BOOKS

When most readers think of books, they are probably thinking of trade books: books intended for the general reader and sold to retail booksellers and libraries (usually public libraries). Trade books can be published in hardcover format, paperback format, or both. They are targeted to every age group from infants (for example, board books) to children to young adults to adults. These are the books that are most often advertised and reviewed in general magazines and newspapers, or discussed on television and radio shows. They may or may not become best-sellers. For all the attention these books receive, however, they do not make up the largest dollar category of publishing; it is estimated that less than 25 percent of the total U.S. dollar volume of book publishing comes from the trade-book category. Furthermore, most of the trade books published in the U.S. are produced by a relative handful of publishers—approximately 200 out of the more than 60,000 publishers listed in the 1999–2000 edition of *Books in Print*.

Trade books are usually further divided into the categories of adult hardcover, adult paperbound, juvenile hardcover, and juvenile paperbound. (The latter two categories may include titles intended for young adult readers, as these books are traditionally issued by the juvenile departments of most trade houses.) Adult trade books are classed as either fiction—general or genre—or nonfiction, but whichever they are, they are usually original works intended for a general audience. It's from this category that the overwhelming majority of the huge best-sellers comes, for instance any new book by John Grisham or Danielle Steel or Stephen King. Altogether, adult trade books accounted for more than three-quarters of the approximately $8 billion worth of trade books sold in 1998. Examples of major players on the trade-publishing scene are Random House, HarperCollins, and G. P. Putnam's.

Juvenile books produce a much smaller percentage of trade revenue than do those intended for adults, accounting for less than 25 percent of dollar volume in trade publishing. There are several reasons for this. One is that far fewer juvenile titles appear each year. Out of the more than 60,000 titles produced in 1998, approximately 4,000 were juvenile books. A second reason is that far fewer copies of juvenile books are printed. Except in the case of a few very well-known authors' works, the original print run of most juvenile titles is less than 5,000 copies, as compared with tens or hundreds of thousands or even a million or more copies of books written for adults. Finally there is much less selling of various subsidiary rights for juvenile books—foreign rights, movie and television rights, reprint rights, and the like. For these reasons, few authors of juvenile books get rich on what they write, but if they are lucky their titles may stay in print for a much longer time than most adult titles. Why are these things so? It's simple. Most juvenile books—some 60 to 75 percent of them, especially hardcovers—are published for the library market. Children themselves rarely buy hardcover books, and adults who buy books for children tend to stick to titles they enjoyed when they were children, such as *Charlotte's Web* or *Winnie the Pooh*, unless a book's author is very popular, such as Maurice Sendak or Beverly Cleary, or the book is a prize winner—a Newbery or Caldecott Medal book, for example.

There are, of course, exceptions. In 1984, Shel Silverstein's collection of poetry for children, *The Light in the Attic*, became the longest-running title in the history of the *New York Times Book Review*'s hardcover best-seller list; in late 1985, a children's picture book, *The Polar Express* by Chris Van Allsburg (a Caldecott Medal winner for an earlier book), first made the *Times* adult fiction best-seller list, and has reappeared with great regularity on that same list during the holiday season ever since. And, in 2000, we have the phenomenon of the Harry Potter books, by British author J. K. Rowland, whose first three books in the series held first, second, and third places on the *New York Times Book Review*'s fiction best-seller list for a number of weeks at the end of 1999, and whose total number of copies in print as of the end of January 2000 exceeded 27 million. While juvenile books may be only a small part of the trade-book picture, and few if any attain the success of the Harry Potter series, many publishers look on them as one of the most consistently profitable segments of trade publishing because they bring in relatively small but steady profit and stay in print much longer than most of their adult trade-book counterparts; the occasional juvenile "blockbuster" provides a little icing on the cake for some publishers and a lodestar for others.

RELIGIOUS BOOKS

Religious books—including bibles, hymnals, prayer books, and books on religious topics—only occasionally appear on any of the standard best-seller lists, but they accounted for more than $1.1 billion in book sales in 1999. Some of these books are published by religious departments of trade publishers; HarperCollins, for example, has long maintained a religious department in San Francisco, but most religious titles are produced by publishers specializing in such endeavors or by religious groups who see their publications as part of their evangelical mission. An example of the former is Thomas Nelson, which for many years claimed to be the world's largest publisher of bibles and which also published many general religious titles. Examples of the latter are the Daughters of St. Paul, Augsburg Fortress (the publishing arm of the American Evangelical Lutheran Church), and the Jewish Publication Society.

Perhaps the largest market for religious books is made up of the estimated 40 million purchasers of fundamentalist Christian books. Books produced by evangelical Christian publishers are sold primarily through some 6,000 religious bookstores in the United States. Until recently, they rarely were sold in general bookstores and even more rarely made standard best-seller lists (although one such title, Tyndale House's *The Living Bible*, has sold nearly 50 million copies since 1971). This situation has changed radically over the last decade, however.

The growth of the Christian book industry since 1975 has been nothing short of phenomenal. While all other segments of publishing were complaining about federal funding cuts for school- and library-book purchases, recessionary trends, and generally flat sales from the mid-1970s to the mid-1990s, sales of Christian books soared as the number of fundamentalist Christians continued to grow during this period, and has leveled off somewhat only since 1995. A contributing factor to this success has been, perhaps ironically, television. Christian television networks beam their messages to the converted all day every day, and the mere mention of a new title (whose author may be a television preacher himself) can ensure very large sales of the book in Christian bookstores.

Even more importantly, these books have made an impression on the non-Christian chain bookstores, which now almost without exception contain good-sized sections usually labeled "Inspirational Books." Because of this phenomenon, book wholesalers now carry large stocks of Christian books for sale to the chains and to their library customers; librarians in the past often resisted purchasing such materials, but they have begun to realize that there are good arguments to be made for meeting the needs of their fundamentalist patrons as well as those of other groups. Finally, such secular book-review journals as *Publishers Weekly*, *Library Journal*, *Booklist*, and *Kirkus Reviews* now routinely review such books and often have sections and even entire issues dedicated to religious books and publishing, with best-seller lists and all, just as they do for other areas of book publishing. *Booklist* even has its own regular column on Christian fiction, edited by John Mort, and it has proven to be very popular with library book selectors. (Readers who are interested in the whole area of Christian publishing will find a wealth of information in Barbara J. Walker's *Developing Christian Fiction Collections for Children and Adults* [1998].)

PROFESSIONAL BOOKS

Professional books are published for and directed at professional people and are specifically related to their work. This category is usually further broken down into four subcategories:

1. Technical/scientific books are written for professionals in the sciences, such as biology, geology, chemistry; or devoted to such technical specialties as engineering, architecture, computer technology, and the like.
2. Medical and health books are intended for health professionals at various levels.
3. Business and other professional books are directed to people in business or management and to members of specific professions that fall outside the technical/scientific/medical categories, such as librarians and accountants.
4. Legal/law books are published by specialized houses for lawyers and other workers in the legal fields.

Like religious-book publishing, this category has grown remarkably over the last two decades as the number of professional people has grown and a large managerial class emerged to meet the needs of an increasingly sophisticated business/economic system. At the same time, students entered the fields of medicine and law in unprecedented numbers, and the need for experts in the whole field of computer technology grew almost exponentially. As a result, since 1972, when about $380 million worth of professional books were sold in the United States, that total has increased to more than $4.4 billion in 1999. Certain astute publishers who slanted most of their books toward this group flourished, and a whole group of new entrepreneurial publishers arose to help fill the needs of the professional class. An example comes from the American Management Association, which observed the increase in numbers of its members at the managerial level and used its contacts and expertise to form its highly successful publishing company, Amacom. On a lighter note, the growth in numbers of personal computer users during the last two decades created a need for simple introductory "how-to-use-my-PC" books, and a company was quickly formed to meet that need. IDG Books Worldwide, Inc., began publishing its "dummies" series (*PCs for Dummies*, *WORD for Windows for Dummies*, and so on) in 1990, and within ten years had 60 million copies of its "dummies" titles in print. Perhaps closer to home, the publisher of this book, Neal-Schuman Publishers Inc., saw the need for librarians to have more materials on library and information science, especially its technological aspects; in 1976 it began publishing books to meet that need, and it hasn't stopped yet.

MASS-MARKET PAPERBACKS

Although paper-covered books have been around in the United States since colonial times, the mass-market paperback as we know it is a relatively modern phenomenon, dating back only to June 1939. In that year, an enterprising publisher, Robert deGraff, decided to produce a line of paperback books that would sell for twenty-five cents each. Although older heads in publishing believed that it was impossible to make a profit at that price, deGraff went ahead. His first list of ten books consisted of reprints of some of the most popular books of the day, including *Lost Horizon*, *The Way of All Flesh*, *The Bridge of San Luis Rey*, *The Murder of Roger Ackroyd*, *Bambi*, *Five Great Tragedies of William Shakespeare*, and Dorothy Parker's *Enough Rope*.

Called Pocket Books, the books were published in a size slightly smaller than today's mass-market paperbacks and had uniformly bright, beautiful covers (although compared to today's brilliant, even gaudy covers, they look a little anemic). The first printing of each title was a conservative 10,000 copies, but to everyone's surprise (except deGraff's) the books took readers by storm, and it was not long before Pocket Books was selling 12,000 to 15,000 copies of deGraff's original list *each day*, even though the books were not distributed "north of Boston, west of Chicago or south of Washington," as *Publishers Weekly* reported in its August 19, 1939, issue.

DeGraff realized that he needed to expand his market to the rest of the country and hit upon a brilliant idea. At the time, magazines and newspapers were distributed by about 800 wholesalers in various territories across the country. These "independent distributors" (IDs), as they called themselves, took on the distribution of Pocket Books to the hundred thousand or so retail outlets they were already supplying with magazines and newspapers. Soon more than three-quarters of Pocket Books' output was being distributed by these IDs, and the books were reaching a "mass market" of readers. (It should be noted here, however, that the term "mass market" in today's publishing parlance refers not to the books reaching the "masses" of readers, but rather to their size, which is just right to fit into the ubiquitous racks found in airports, drugstores, chain bookstores—all over—in the United States and Canada.)

The success of deGraff's operation soon led to imitators, and over the next few years other mass-market publishing companies were formed, among them Avon Books, Penguin Books (long published in Great Britain, but only in the United States since the early 1940s), Bantam Books, and others, many of which still survive today, and most of which are still distributed primarily by IDs, with the rest sold to bookstores and libraries in particular by book wholesalers. As far as these books go, the only big difference between 1939 and 1999 may be in the growth of mass-market publishing in the six decades of its existence. Today the rack-sized, mass-market book accounts for more than $1.5 billion in sales in the United States, so it is fairly safe to say that the format is here to stay.

UNIVERSITY PRESSES

The fewer than 100 university presses that publish books in the United States account for only a small percentage of the total titles published, but the books' influence and importance are often disproportionate to their numbers. A great deal of what is published by the university presses is vital to the scholarly community as a means of disseminating information that might otherwise be lost. But because the scholarly community is small, university presses usually publish in very small quantities; a press run may range from a few hundred copies (or even a few dozen) to a maximum of a few thousand copies, and most of these will be sold to academic, special, and public libraries, and to scholars and specialists.

Only occasionally will a university press publish a "best-seller"; one example is Louisiana State University Press's publication a few decades ago of John Kennedy Toole's posthumous novel, *A Confederacy of Dunces*, which promptly made a number of national best-seller lists and also received a number of literary prizes. And, of course, the University of Chicago's *Manual of Style* has sold hundreds of thousands of copies through many printings and is still going strong. For the most part, however, these are the exceptions to the rule, and most titles have enough copies printed to meet the needs of libraries, scholars, and specialists, and that is all. It is the very limited size of this market that keeps trade publishers from going after it, but it's that very fact that allows the university presses to stay alive.

There are signs, however, that the picture is changing. Over the last two decades university presses have attempted to broaden their audience, going beyond scholars to a more general, though still highly literate, readership. The number of titles being published each year increased over the last decade from about 3,600 titles in 1987 to some 4,000 in 1999. University presses have also concentrated more on regional trade publishing, a category that comprises up to 40 percent of some lists, and they have gained a reputation for fine translation not only in the areas of fiction and poetry, but also, increasingly, of non-fiction. They have also secured reprint rights to many top-quality commercial books (Gayle Feldman, "University Presses: A Changing Role," *Publishers Weekly*, September 23, 1988), and continue to do so.

In the past, most university presses were subsidized by the sponsoring university (or learned society or museum), thus making it possible for them to stay in existence even with such a limited market. This has changed significantly in the last few years. Today most are expected to be at least self-supporting, even if nonprofit. This has largely been achieved by astute management and stricter controls over what is published, backed up by the rigorous standards set by the presses' professional organization, the Association of American University Presses (AAUP). Both tactics have helped the great majority to weather the period of financial stress that has affected most American universities as a result of declining enrollment.

TEXTBOOK PUBLISHING

Publishing of textbooks from elementary school through college/university level comprises the largest category of publishing, accounting for more than $6 billion in sales out of a total publishing dollar value of about $26 billion. Most are produced by houses specializing in this type of publishing, although some trade publishers have traditionally operated textbook divisions, some of which earn more for the parent company than their trade division counterparts; most trade publishers today are selling off their textbook operations for purely economic reasons, however.

Once one of the most lucrative of all kinds of publishing, textbook publishing has faced some real problems over the last few decades. For one thing, the huge infusion of federal money into the schools during the 1960s and early 1970s has disappeared for all intents and purposes and shows no signs of ever being replaced. A drop in the birth rate has reduced enrollment in schools, colleges, and universities, and so fewer textbooks are needed. Urban schools have special problems that make the headlines regularly, not the least of which is a lack of money for everything, including textbooks. Finally, the halcyon days of statewide adoption of a few texts mandated for use in all schools in the state are long over. A few states, such as Texas and California, still engage in the practice of text adoption, but those that do recommend a broader range of texts, giving educators some choice. As a result, few textbook publishers are guaranteed a sale of perhaps several hundred thousand copies of a given text annually as they often were in the past, and thus, considering the initial inordinately high cost of launching a new text or series of textbooks, this kind of publishing has become an extremely high-risk business indeed.

SUBSCRIPTION REFERENCE BOOKS

There are probably few older adults in the United States who have not been approached at one time or another by one of the thousands of salespeople who sold subscription reference books, primarily sets of encyclopedias. At one time in the recent past, more than 90 percent of all such sales were made directly to homes or through the mail; the remainder were and still are sold directly to libraries and schools but rarely to retail booksellers. (Today these books are still sold to individuals and families for home use, but the coming of personal computers has radically changed the market for book reference materials. A family wanting a new encyclopedia in the year 2000 is much more likely to buy an electronic version on CD-ROM than a print version.)

Because of the nature of subscription reference book publishing, whatever its format, only a few companies have managed to produce the sets at a profit, and so it is very uncommon to see a new series or set launched. First, the initial investment in time and money to produce, for example, a new multivolume encyclopedia is astronomical. If the set is to compete in a highly competitive marketplace, it must be authoritative, which means that experts in hundreds or even thousands of fields must be hired to write everything from one-paragraph entries to major articles on the most esoteric subjects. Further investment must be made in the experts who design and produce the books or CD-ROMs; in the cost of ink, paper, binders, and other materials needed for a set of a dozen or more volumes; in the photographers whose work usually illustrates such works, and the mapmakers and other graphic artists whose work clarifies the text; and in the massive promotion program required for a publisher to break into this market. Finally, most such works, if they are at all reliable, are updated annually, which means that a large share of the profits must be plowed back into the business each year. As a result of these factors, only one major set of encyclopedias has been introduced in the United States over the last twenty-five years, *The Academic American Encyclopedia*, which, after a somewhat rocky start, seems to have established itself. The real phenomenon of the late 1990s, however, is the enormous success of encyclopedia publishing in CD-ROM format. Half a dozen publishers vie to have their CDs preloaded into personal computers; probably the most successful of these is Microsoft's *Encarta*, but *Compton's*, *Britannica*, and others are not far behind. For those who do not have the preloaded software on a new PC, many choices at very reasonable prices, compared to the older, boundbook versions, are available in various kinds of stores; *Encyclopaedia Britannica* is one example, selling on the Internet in April 2000 for $49.95. (For more and valuable information on encyclopedias in both formats, print and CD-ROM, *Booklist* annually runs a major section devoted to analysis and ratings of new and revised encyclopedias.)

MAIL-ORDER PUBLISHING

While it is of course possible for any kind of book to be sold by mail, mail-order publishing as the AAP defines it refers to a very specialized kind of publishing, one that has its origins in the magazine-publishing industry. The AAP uses the term to refer to books intended to be sold to the general consumer through mail-order advertising and marketing on a mass basis. Mail-order publishers use their own mailing lists or they purchase or rent specific mailing lists they have rated as a source of potential customers; they mail out hundreds of thousands, even millions, of brightly colored, slick brochures to these potential customers in the hope of getting a 1 or 2 percent response.

Like subscription reference book marketing, mail-order publishing is a high-risk endeavor not only because of the amount of "front money" necessary to design, print, and mail all those brochures, but also because the recipients are not necessarily book buyers and may resist the high price tag that mail-order books must of necessity command. Nevertheless, a shrewd advertising campaign coupled with a carefully selected mailing list can sell hundreds of thousands of books. It is just this kind of approach that made Time-Life Publishing one of the nation's largest publishers a decade or so ago, using its subscription lists from its *Time* and *Life* subscribers as a target for selling its hardcover series books, and that company's success led other companies to seek a share of this nearly half a billion dollar a year business. A current example of a company that followed Time-Life's successful mail-order marketing techniques is Rodale Press, established in 1932 and long a publisher of health, self-help, and gardening books, and of two magazines, one dedicated to organic gardening and one to holistic health—*Organic Gardening* and *Prevention*, respectively. While Rodale's books were always successfully sold to wholesalers and retailers, the company enjoyed its greatest sales from bombarding its magazine customers (and potential customers from other mailing lists it carefully selected and purchased) with colorful, attractive brochures offering the books by mail on an installment plan, with a money-back offer if customers weren't satisfied; to say this ploy was successful is an understatement, to say the least.

BOOK CLUBS

Though the mail-order book business per se is relatively large, another type of marketing books through the mail is even larger, exceeding mail ordering by more than $300 million annually. Book clubs provide a method for many people to get books relatively easily without having to think much about it; often, they save money, too. The two giants of the industry are familiar to anyone who reads magazines, because it is through that medium that book clubs market their wares: Book-of-the-Month Club and its paperback arm, the Quality Paperback Book Club; and Literary Guild, owned by Doubleday (at the time of this writing, the book-trade journals were announcing that BOMC and Literary Guild were merging). But there are hundreds of other book clubs that cater to a multiplicity of special interests, from the Mystery Book Club, the Science Fiction Book Club, the History Book Club, and the Military Book Club, to such rather more esoteric offerings as those of the Erotic Book Society, the Secretary's Book Club, and the Book Club for Poetry. In recent years book clubs that cater to reader groups among the professions have proliferated—the Lawyer's Book Club and the Builders' and Contractors' Book Society, for example. Scholastic has long had the edge in such children's paperback book clubs as Arrow Book Club; the fact that they have been able to market these books in and through schools has been a major factor in Scholastic's success in this area.

Whatever the interest group served, book clubs have been a success from their beginnings in the 1920s, when Book of the Month and Literary Guild first saw the light of day. Even then, when far fewer books were published, there were still too many for the average purchaser to choose from, and customers/members appreciated both the preselection of good books by the clubs and their substantial savings, as well as the bonuses frequently offered. Today, when a bookstore (usually a chain store) can be found in nearly every shopping mall in the country, millions of readers still depend on the clubs to provide their reading material, so, despite the ups and downs that have been the fate of other segments of the book industry, the book clubs have remained both stable and profitable.

THE INDEPENDENTS

The R. R. Bowker Company, which keeps many statistical records on the publishing industry, indicates that between 1970 and 1999 the number of U.S. publishers increased by about tenfold, from 6,000 to approximately 60,000; even that figure may be low, since Bowker tracks only those publishers that provide records of their output for inclusion in Bowker's many databases and publications. This is particularly surprising because the number of trade, mass-market paperback, university press, and textbook publishers actually decreased during this period, but there is a valid reason for the increase overall, and that is the enormous growth and vitality of the small presses, often referred to as "independent" or "alternative" publishers.

The thousands of titles produced each year by these presses range from avant garde literary works to self-help books, from books with countercultural tone or theme, to fad books and books for highly specialized interest groups such as survivalists, who depend on an independent publisher such as Paladin Press to provide them with information on how to survive in the wilderness or garrote an attacker.

Many alternative-press books are characterized by the aesthetic quality of their design and manufacture as well as by their content. For example, a very small New England company, Lime Rock Press, has turned out a number of exquisitely bound miniature books; Peter Pauper Press has been producing elegant editions of shorter classics such as *The Rubaiyat of Omar Khaayam* for decades at extremely reasonable prices. Other presses produce limited, signed editions of certain authors for sale to collectors. For example, Stephen King's *Skeleton Crew* was published by a small press in a limited, signed edition of 1,000 copies at $75 per copy; within two months it was sold out and used copies were commanding more than $1,000 each. Other presses' output may be printed on fairly primitive equipment so that prices can be held down; the books they produce may look amateurish at best, but they can have a powerful impact. The original edition of *Our Bodies, Ourselves*, for example, was mimeographed and stapled together by its publisher, the Boston Women's Health Collective, and sold for thirty-five cents. Through word of mouth alone it became an underground best-seller and was later picked up by a trade publisher, Simon & Schuster. Some forty years later it has sold millions of copies and is still in print and still selling.

Whatever their format and content, small-press books are usually books that trade publishers did not want to publish or that their authors did not want trade publishers to produce. They are often labors of love, and frequently reflect their publishers' intent to provide the reading public with information not available from the larger, established houses. As such, they can give vitality, currency, and depth to a library's collection, and should be treated with the respect they deserve, even though librarians may sometimes have to make a special effort to search out and obtain them.

VANITY/SUBSIDY PUBLISHING

For the writer who just can't get published by anyone and who has some money to spend, a half-dozen or so publishers specialize in what is referred to in the book trade as "vanity" publishing. It is just what the name implies. No matter how ridiculous the writer's thesis or how dreadful his or her style, for a fee that ranges from a few thousand dollars to three or four times that much, the vanity publisher will produce a bound book from the author's manuscript and make an attempt, however desultory, to market it.

Many of these titles find their way into libraries, usually as gifts from the author, who soon discovers that he or she has hundreds of copies on hand either because of the content or because the books are poorly bound, may be almost primitively illustrated, or just plain have proved to be of little or no interest to anyone except the author and family and friends. Uncritical acceptance of such gifts is usually a mistake and can seriously weaken the library's collection, although there may be an occasion when a local author's work can be useful in a library for public relations purposes or because of the local nature of the topic. As a rule, however, the same collection-development guidelines should be used regarding acceptance of vanity titles as are used for any other kind of gifts.

REPRINTING

Of the 60,000 or so titles published annually in the United States, more than half will be out of print within six months to a year of their publication date. While many books may richly deserve such a fate, some do not, and this is where the reprinter comes in. For example, it was almost impossible to find hardcover copies of many classics of American literature until the late 1970s, when Library of America, a specialized publisher, began reprinting handsome hardcover versions of such classics, managing at the same time to turn a profit. A few other publishers followed suit, among them Random House, which revived the almost defunct Modern Library series (which at one time had been the largest-selling classics line in the country). Another company, Dodd, Mead (since defunct), gave new life to Agatha Christie's enormously and eternally popular mysteries in hardcover, and a few other publishers have followed suit.

Another specialized and very successful area of reprinting is in large-type books. Estimates of the number of visually handicapped persons in the United States range from 20 million to as high as 35 million, and the large-type book gives many of those people who retain a modicum of vision the ability to read a hardcover or paperback edition without a magnifying glass. Librarians purchase most of the output of the half-dozen or so major large-type reprinters and often find that these books are among the most frequently circulated items in their collections.

Finally, advances in book-production technology have made possible another kind of reprinting, called on-demand printing, which allows the vendor to produce one or more copies of a title that may be out of print or in the public domain within hours of an order for it—if, of course, it has been entered into the vendor's database. Supporters claim that with on-demand printing, it is possible that no book may ever go out of print in the future, but time alone will tell whether or not this will happen.

OTHER KINDS OF PUBLISHING

No discussion of book publishing in the United States would be complete without mention of the enormous number of publications generated by government agencies—federal, state, and local—or of the extensive output of the thousands of societies and associations that produce books for their particular constituencies. The largest of the former, of course, is the Government Printing Office (GPO), which is often and rightfully referred to as the world's largest publisher, but government units at the state, county, and local levels also publish a great deal. Societies and associations as publishers range from the local historical society publishing books of local or regional interest to an association such as the American Management Association with its AMACOM line of books for managers and would-be managers, or the International Fire Protection Association's extensive list of fire prevention and control publications.

THE LIBRARIAN'S CHALLENGE

It's obvious that the librarian involved with the selection, collection building, and acquisitions processes faces a bewildering proliferation of sources for materials. The problem of obtaining books becomes further exacerbated by the fact that each publishing house, each society, each association is unique in its approach to marketing, pricing and discounting, and distributing its products. For these reasons a working, if rudimentary, knowledge of publishing's idiosyncrasies is crucial to developing library collections. The librarian who buys materials in an intelligent and timely manner based on such knowledge will find the whole business both challenging and exciting, and will earn the gratitude of colleagues who select books and build collections. The ultimate—and perhaps the most important—result will be a community of satisfied library patrons. And that, after all, is what libraries are all about.

3 CREATING A BOOK

> We speak of book publishing as an industry and a profession. Both designations are certainly appropriate. Book publishing is a business conducted, for the most part, for profit. But its practitioners—at least those who do it honor—have motivations that transcend their profit interests. They know that books are no mere commodity, no mere items for consumption that leave their readers much as they find them. Books, like other vehicles of information and sources of entertainment, can change, influence, elevate, demean, exalt, or depress those who expose themselves to them. What books are and can be depends heavily on the judgment, integrity, taste, and acumen of those who select and produce them—their publishers.
>
> John P. Dessauer, *Book Publishing: What It Is, What It Does*

Whether book publishing is an industry, a profession, or even an art is perhaps moot to the librarian who is interested only in the end result of the publishing process, the book. Yet if librarians are to be informed and intelligent purchasers of books, they must have some idea of the publishing industry's workings. They must understand why so many books are published (even though more than three-quarters of them do not pay for themselves), why books that are published cost so much, and why so many titles go out of print so fast. A brief look at the complexity of the entire publishing process can give some insight into these three questions as well as other factors that affect our ability to provide books for library patrons.

It takes just as much time to produce the average book as it does to produce the average human baby: about nine months. The book-production process is tedious, involving dozens, even hundreds, of people and a set of complex but necessary operations. It is an extremely high-risk endeavor, requiring substantial initial cash outlays on the part of the risk-taker (the publisher) for months or even years before the completed book sees the light of day, much less begins to earn a profit—if it ever does. This entire process begins, of course, with a writer and, if all goes well, ends with a reader. From one end of this continuum to the other lies a fascinating process: the creation of a book.

Every book, be it fiction or nonfiction, begins as an idea in a writer's mind. The idea may have originated with the writer, who wishes others to hear it, or may have been someone else's, someone who does not wish to or cannot express the idea on paper and who approaches the writer to do just that. In either case, the writer is the teller of the tale, and in that sense is the first real link in the chain of events that leads from idea to finished book.

Those who have heard writers speak about their work know that each writer's method is different. Some write in offices in their homes, others settle for the dining room table. Some write in longhand, correcting and revising as they go. A few may still use a typewriter, but most others now compose on a word processor or personal computer. Some go at the writing full tilt, creating a first draft over a period of time, and then revise and rewrite the draft. Others write a page or two a day, or so many pages a day, or a chapter a week. Yet others do not put a word of the book itself on paper until a detailed outline of the entire work is completed. Some write for a few hours a day, some only at certain times of the day or night. Some writers can turn out a manuscript—or two or three—a year; others may work on a single book for several years, even decades.

Whatever the writer's method, the goal is to sooner or later have a completed manuscript for a book neatly typed and ready to offer to a publisher. In general, the writer submits either a manuscript or a book proposal to a particular publisher or sends it to a literary agent, who then submits it to the publisher judged most likely to be interested in the work—all for a percentage (usually 10 percent) of the monies ultimately realized from the sale of the published book.

In some cases, the author may be in the happy position of already having a publisher interested in accepting the manuscript upon completion. If the author's earlier work is known, the publisher may offer a contract for the writer's next book or books even before they are begun, or on the basis of a chapter or an outline. Or the publisher may commission a book on a given subject because of the writer's expertise in or knowledge of a certain field or subject; most technical, professional, and scientific books, and nearly all textbooks, are produced in this way.

If a publisher accepts the author's manuscript (or idea for a book), the author is usually offered a contract for a royalty, or percentage of the money received from sales. Occasionally, publishers pay an author an advance—a sum of money that is subtracted from whatever royalties are earned once the book begins to sell. Once a contract is signed, however, the decision to go ahead with publication is made on the basis of whether the final manuscript is acceptable. If it is not, the author must either work on it until it is, or return any advances to the publisher.

THE PUBLISHER

Regardless of how the manuscript has been submitted—by author or by agent—once it is in the hands of a publishing house nearly all decisions regarding the potential book's future are out of the hands of its creator, the writer. The first of these decisions is whether the manuscript is publishable. Publishing houses, especially trade houses, receive thousands of manuscripts each year; only an extremely small percentage of them ever reach book stage. Doubleday, for example, once claimed to receive about 10,000 *unsolicited* manuscripts each year and to publish just three or four of them at best in a given year.

Most of these unsolicited manuscripts are submitted by authors themselves. Smart authors research the latest edition of *Writer's Market* or *Literary Market Place* to determine which house is most likely to accept their manuscript. If the potential book is fiction, for example, the author wants to identify those houses that publish a lot of fiction or that specialize in certain fiction genres—such as mysteries, science fiction, or gothic romances. *Writer's Market*, in fact, contains not only detailed listings of many publishers' current needs or wants, but also what they do *not* need or want; so if an entry therein notes that X Publishers is not accepting fantasy, for example, the writer of a Tolkien-type quest novel would be wise not to submit it there. Another important piece of information offered in *Writer's Market* is whether a given publisher accepts unsolicited manuscripts (and most do not) or requires submission by an agent. The writer who ignores this basic stricture is wasting everyone's time.

Assuming that the manuscript has been properly submitted, it receives the first in a series of readings. This is usually done by an employee of the house known as a first reader (some publishers farm manuscripts out to freelance readers; in other houses the editors read the submissions themselves), who makes a judgment as to whether the manuscript should be passed on to an editor for further consideration or should be rejected and returned to the author. If it is not rejected, it is read by an editor or a succession of editors, each of whom has some say as to whether it is worth publishing and whether it will earn a profit if it is published. Others in the house who may also be asked for an opinion are the publisher's sales and promotion, marketing, and subsidiary-rights staff. If these people are unconvinced of a potential book's salability, this may affect the publishing decision as much as the editor's judgment.

Certain questions are given serious consideration before a contract is offered to the author, among them:

- *editorial considerations.* How well written is the manuscript? Does it read well? Will it require lengthy (and costly) copy editing? Has the publishing house (or other publishing houses) published anything too similar to this manuscript already? Does it fit into the publisher's present or future lists? Is the author known to the reading public and other potential purchasers/users of the book? Is the book's topic timely? Is its information accurate?
- *costs.* Will production costs be reasonable, or will they be so high that the book probably won't earn a profit? Is the book likely to earn a profit upon publication, or is it more likely to be profitable only over the long term? How much of an advance will the author require? What percentage will his or her royalty be?
- *marketing.* What is the book's intended or potential audience? How will it be promoted? How much will be invested in its promotion and marketing? What price will be charged for it? What will be its first print run—a few thousand or a few hundred thousand? What are this book's chances for sale of subsidiary rights, as in to foreign markets, for mass-market or large-type reprint, for movie or television tie-ins, for serialization or excerpting in magazines, and the like?

Even the most careful analysis of all these factors does not guarantee that a book will sell enough copies to break even, much less make a profit. In a sense, publishers take a calculated risk on every book they finally decide to publish; sometimes it pays off, and sometimes it doesn't. Trade publishers claim that only 20 percent of the titles they issue pay for themselves. That 20 percent is crucial, however, because it can make the difference between staying in business and going broke. A reliable, well-known, and prolific author—a John Grisham, a Stephen King, a Danielle Steel—can do a great deal to make up for the losses incurred by the failure of the 80 percent of a publisher's list that doesn't make it, and this is part of the game; but anyone who is not a born risk-taker should probably never even attempt to become a publisher. The possibilities for success are there, but the probability of failure makes book publishing a very risky endeavor indeed.

FROM MANUSCRIPT TO BOOK

Once the decision to publish has been made, work begins on turning the manuscript into a book. The first step is the editor's, who does everything possible to improve the manuscript: pointing out its defects and suggesting ways for the author to remedy them, looking for inconsistencies and contradictions, and correcting obvious minor problems such as spelling and punctuation. In the case of illustrated books, the editor must be certain that photos, charts, or drawings are placed in the text at the appropriate places and that the proper captions accompany them. If necessary, the editor also checks on the material that appears before and after the body of the text (front and back matter), such as the title page, copyright page, table of contents, appendices, indexes, and so on. Finally, the editor fills out a manuscript transmittal form detailing all the information available about the book: title, author, editor, proposed number of pages, quantity of copies wanted, front and back matter, illustrations, any special matter, jacket copy and art, publication date, tentative price, and any other pertinent data. This form accompanies the manuscript and is the master guide for all others who will work at making it into a book. The editor then sends the manuscript along with the form to a copy editor, whose job it is to give the manuscript a final check for errors of any kind, to "style" it, and to give it a final careful check for spelling, consistency, and usage. Once this has been done, the manuscript is given over to those who will design and produce the book.

BOOK DESIGN

The designer reads the manuscript carefully with one purpose in mind: to translate what the author has done with words into a visual image of what the book should finally look like while staying within the budgetary limits set for the book. Every detail of the book's appearance is planned, from the paper it is printed on to typefaces, to how the title page looks and how much space ("leading") appears between the lines of type, to the design of the running heads (words that appear at the top of each page of text), to how variants of the text itself (such as quoted material or lines of poetry) will look throughout the text.

A specification sheet is drawn up giving detailed plans for all sections of the book, from front matter through the text to back matter, and is sent with the manuscript on to the production department. The production department contracts for and supervises the manufacturing of the book, including composition (typesetting) and printing.

The one aspect of a book's design that generally is not controlled by the designer is the jacket design, which is usually assigned by the house's art director to an artist who specializes in book covers. Because the jacket is looked upon primarily as a selling tool for the book, the marketing department also gets involved. A successful jacket can enhance a book's sales, just as a successful television commercial can increase the sales of aspirin or automobiles. In the case of mass-market paperbacks, a striking cover design can cause a potential buyer to pull the book off the rack and look at it—the first step toward purchasing it in our impulse-buying, image-conscious world.

PRODUCTION

Once the bulk of the designer's work has been done, the production department takes over. Usually a production supervisor, who may have several assistants, coordinates the many steps involved in producing the book. This person contacts compositors, suppliers (of paper, binders' board, and the like), and printers for competitive bids, and oversees the entire production process so that the finished book is available to coincide with its scheduled publication date and accompanying promotional plans.

At the same time, the production supervisor is responsible for effecting whatever economies will keep costs down. Ordering enough paper for several books at a time, for example, results in a better price for the paper than would ordering separate lots for each book; this is an important consideration, since paper is one of the biggest costs in book manufacturing. The head of production also consults frequently with the book's printer and binder to ensure that schedules are being followed, that design instructions are being observed, and that costs do not exceed projections.

PUBLICITY AND SALES

PUBLICITY

During the lengthy production process, several other important activities are going on in the publishing house. Publicity, promotion, and sales staffs are doing everything they can to ensure that the books will reach their widest possible audience—in other words, that they will sell.

Long before the books are offered for sale, the process of publicizing them begins. It is the job of the publicity department to stimulate interest in the forthcoming book so that potential purchasers—be they bookstores, wholesalers, libraries, or others (perhaps general readers or students)—will be anxious to obtain copies as soon as they are available. Toward this end, the publicity department prepares copy for the publisher's new catalog, which announces and describes each forthcoming title and whatever special promotions will accompany it. It also prepares announcements of the book's publication, which are sent to people whose remarks can affect the book's sales. These include newspaper and magazine book-review editors, editors of journals that announce new publications (such as *Publishers Weekly*), or influential people, frequently other authors, whose comments on the book—favorable of course—are used to advertise the book. In fact, many tales have been told about how ingenious publicity departments can use such quotes even when they are unfavorable. A statement such as "Stunning in its awfulness!" may be excerpted to "Stunning . . . !" (For an amusing discussion by someone who is frequently asked to comment on books before their publication date, see Susan Brownmiller's " 'A Word from You'—Confessions of an Ex-Blurb Writer" in *The New York Times Book Review*, January 12, 1983, p.3.)

A second major part of the publicity effort is getting the book reviewed in appropriate journals. If timeliness of the review is a factor, the publicity staff may elect to send bound galleys—sets of galley proofs cut to page size—to selected editors and reviewers with the hope that they will review the book before its publication date. A secondary bonus from this is, of course, more quotes for the publicity department to use in advertisements.

Books or galleys may also be sent to television and radio personalities who discuss books on a regular basis or who interview authors. Television talk-show star Oprah Winfrey, for example, can assure thousands of sales of a book few people have ever heard of simply by discussing it or featuring it on her extremely popular show. National Public Radio has helped sell many a book that has been discussed on its different shows. This is one of the most successful ways of promoting books by well-known authors, but it can also be effective for a very provocative book by an unknown. Some authors may be sent on promotional tours to carefully chosen cities; to autograph parties in bookstores, schools, or libraries; or to "author talks" at meetings and conventions. And one of the newest and perhaps best kinds of publicity comes from having a book listed prominently or reviewed briefly on an online bookseller's Website; Amazon.com, for example, the largest of these, can stimulate sales almost as well as Oprah can (although there is increasing questioning of why and how certain books are featured there so prominently and others never appear at all).

No one way of promoting books is best for all books, but any method that gets the potential customer interested enough in a book to purchase it is considered effective. For library book purchasers, however, reviews usually are considered the most important factor in the buy/don't buy decision. Librarians, even those working in the largest institutions, can purchase only a small percentage of the tens of thousands of titles published each year, and so reviews become vitally important in the selection process. However, the librarian must remember that only a few thousand out of those tens of thousands of titles are reviewed at all; of the 60,000 titles published in the United States in 1998, for example, *Booklist* reviewed only 4,206 adult and 2,277 juvenile titles, *Publishers Weekly* reviewed 5,576 adult and 2,076 juvenile titles, and *Library Journal* covered 5,723 adult books—and of course there was considerable overlap of titles reviewed among the journals. But judicious monitoring of ads, announcements, and other promotional items can help the librarian make some good choices from books that are not reviewed, and can result in a stronger, broader collection than one that is composed only of books that *have* been reviewed.

SALES

The next-to-the-last step in the publishing process is actually selling the book, whether the ultimate customer is a retailer, a wholesaler, a library, a school, or an individual book buyer. Many publishing houses have a sales staff whose job it is simply to peddle the house's wares. Others use independent representatives in various areas of the country who usually sell several houses' lines on a purely commission basis. The extraordinarily high cost of keeping house salespeople on the road (currently estimated at $275 per day)—plus paying their salaries, commissions, and bonuses—makes using independent, commission-only reps an increasingly attractive alternative.

Armed with information about the publisher's new line, including catalogs and other promotional materials, the salesperson visits bookstores, wholesalers, schools, libraries, and other potential customers to describe forthcoming titles and take orders for them. The order is important to the salesperson, but is perhaps even more important to the publisher. An unusually large number of pre-publication-date orders, for example, may prompt the publisher to increase a book's initial print run—or to do the opposite, if orders seem too few. An example can be seen in a title that was the third book in author Jean Auel's enormously popular prehistoric saga, *The Mammoth Hunters*. Based on the sales of its two predecessor titles, Crown had conservatively scheduled a first print run of 750,000 copies, but prepublication orders were so large that the first printing was increased to one million copies—a new record for a first printing. The final total of hardcover copies of the book sold in 1985 exceeded one-and-a-half million. A more current example is an autobiography by a professional wrestler, Mick Foley, *Have a Nice Day!*, published by HarperCollins in 1999. It was originally scheduled for only a few thousand copies in its first printing, but that was increased tenfold on the basis of prepublication orders, and the book made the *New York Times* best-seller list, where it remained for the rest of 1999 and well into 2000.

The importance of the sales rep to the success or failure of a book is perhaps most obvious in sales to the retail sector and to the large whole-saler. If a big chain such as Barnes & Noble or a major wholesaler such as Ingram or Baker & Taylor can be persuaded to buy several hundred thousand copies of a book, for example, its success is virtu-ally assured. In addition, publishers can stimulate further interest in the book by quoting these very large sales figures in their subsequent advertising, thus encouraging others to "get on the bandwagon," as it were.

For the library book purchaser, however, the sales call may be less effective; few conscientious librarians will buy a disproportionate num-ber of Viking Press titles, for example, simply because the Viking sales-person makes a good pitch. Most librarians tend to be title-by-title purchasers, not "house-line" purchasers; a sales call to a library may not be nearly as effective as a review or even an ad for a book. (There are exceptions, of course. One highly successful children's book rep in my state frequently boasts that certain schools and school libraries spend their entire book budgets on his line, simply because he is the only sales rep who bothers to call on remote, small accounts; they are so grateful for the attention that they give him all their business! One can only wonder what their collections look like.)

At long last, the book is ready to ship. The legions of people who have labored long and hard to bring it to this point have largely fin-ished their work; their success depends on whether the book seems attractive enough or important enough so that the customer will buy it. At this point, there is really only one more obstacle for the pub-lisher to overcome: distribution of the books to their appropriate mar-kets. While this may seem like the simplest step in the long process of a book's evolution, it is probably the most crucial step in the whole process, so crucial that the AAP's Book Industry Study Group (BISG)—whose members are from publishing, wholesaling, bookselling, and librarianship—has labeled it the most serious problem facing the in-dustry in this century. Because it is so important, not only to publish-ers but also to librarians, the next chapter examines the book distribution process in the United States and its impact on library book purchasing.

4 BOOK DISTRIBUTION

> The distribution system of the [publishing] industry . . . is unsystematized, underdeveloped, ineffective, unprofitable and static.
>
> O. H. Cheney, in a publishing industry-commissioned report to the National Association of Book Publishers, 1931.

> Unfortunately, most of the problems related to book distribution that Cheney delineated more than 50 years ago still exist today.
>
> *The Future of the Book*, a report prepared by SKP Associates for the Center for the Book, Library of Congress, published by UNESCO, 1984.

> That chaos has pervaded the book industry in the last three years is evident enough. *Massive returns* and the decline of independent booksellers are merely two symptoms of an industry searching to find itself. [emphasis added]
>
> Paul Hilts and James Lichtenberg, "Redefining Distribution"

Book distribution is much more complex than just shipping cartons of books from the publisher's warehouse to a designated destination such as a bookstore or a library. Perhaps because of its complexity, it has proved resistant to the industry's best efforts to simplify or improve it.

In an article published in the October 22, 1982, issue of *Publishers Weekly* (*PW*), T. J. Greene enumerated some "financial strategies for hard times"—strategies that publishers, facing a drop in book sales even as book prices soared, felt were necessary for survival. The strategies included production economies such as using lighter weight paper, smaller typefaces, less expensive cover stock and forms of binding, and other similar measures. Tighter controls on other expenses were also suggested: cutting back on participation in trade shows, conventions, and association meetings; cutting travel budgets and costs; reducing the size of advances to authors; moving publishing offices to areas less expensive than New York; and establishing tighter control of cash flow. What it all added up to was advising publishers to do what they have always done in hard times, and even in good times: to raise book prices and attempt to cut costs in essentially minor areas, while ignoring the most costly area of all, the book-distribution process.

Eight weeks later, *Publishers Weekly* published another article (December 17, 1982) entitled "Moving Books Around," in which Joseph Deitch stated:

> The complexities and cost considerations involved in shipping books to customers are getting increasingly high-level attention from publishers in these parlous times. . . . [Publishing houses are taking] a fresh look at what many now regard as the industry's second most important function: getting books to customers at lower prices, more rapidly, and with less chance of damage.

Deitch went on to describe the distribution policies and strategies of a number of publishers, from warehousing to shipping and invoicing, and what they were doing to minimize costs in this vital area. Hilts and Lichtenberg, quoted above in *PW* sixteen years later, essentially reiterated what Cheney, SKP Associates, and Deitch had said, once again bemoaning the book-distribution process, particularly its returns aspect (of which more later in this chapter). In March 1998, in an article in the journal *Modern Materials Handling*, a spokesman for Von Holtzbrinck Publishing Services, owner of a number of American publishing houses, said of the book distribution process, "Book distribution has been a costly, labor intensive business resistant to modernization. . . . Von Holtzbrinck is out to change that. . . . Our goal: cut distribution costs." The company planned to do this by building the most automated book-distribution center in the world, at a cost of $30 million; the facility was completed in 1999.

THE BISG STUDIES

In 1967, the AAP's Book Industry Study Group (BISG) surveyed its membership's leaders to elicit, among other things, which areas of book publishing they felt were in most need of study and research. Book distribution was a primary area identified by all groups. Fourteen years later BISG finally commissioned the independent research organization Arthur Andersen & Company to conduct a study of the book-distribution process in the United States.

The results of the Andersen survey were published in 1982 as *Book*

Distribution in the United States: Issues and Perceptions. The findings revealed little that Cheney's 1931 study had not discovered:

> The physical distribution system . . . has experienced unabated cost pressures. Labor, capital, energy, and postal cost increases have been substantial. Changing marketing practices and consumer buying patterns, in some market segments, have contributed to escalating book returns with their inherent wastefulness. . . . Recent consumer research in the industry indicates that improvement in the efficiency of the physical distribution system is an important, if not key factor in meeting the ever more diverse consumer demands in a more timely manner. That, in turn, is an essential ingredient for the [book] industry's growth.

One major "new" finding was that if the process were ever to be improved, publishers would, of necessity, have to initiate the improvement themselves. (One can only wonder who else could initiate it.) A second, perhaps more valid finding was that respondees felt that the (then) new electronic technologies might make such improvement possible where it had not been possible in the past. Whether that has proven to be the case, however, is still an open question some eighteen years after the Andersen study. If one follows the ongoing travails of the industry over that period, it appears that there has been little more than the "same old same old" occurring, electronic technologies or not, with one notable exception: the Von Holtzbrinck center mentioned above.

SALES REPS AND ADVANCE SALES

Distributing books is a process that ranges from the simple task of sending out galleys to reviewers, to the disheartening task of selling off unsold copies. For purposes of this discussion, the process begins with receipt of an order in a publishing house and ends in the sale of books to remainder dealers. But even this makes the process sound simple—or at least defined. In fact, however, so many aspects are dependent on each other that it's hard to separate them for an objective look.

The only "hard" information publishers have on which to base a decision about how many copies of a book to print and how much money to set aside for advertising comes from reports of advance sales drummed up by sales reps in the field. But just how "hard" is this information? Not very, in most cases, and the culprit is the book industry's publishing cycle, which bears no relation to objective reality but is instead tied to the practice of publishers holding two sales conferences for reps each year. These meetings are spent familiarizing the company's reps with the new products they will be selling over the course of the year. For example, anyone who reads *Publishers Weekly*, *Library Journal*, or other book-oriented journals is aware of each year's adult book-announcement issues. The biggest is devoted to announcements of books to be published in the fall of the year because of the possibility of high sales levels during the Christmas season. These big issues are intended, of course, to inform retail customers about the titles the reps learned about at their fall sales meeting. The fall announcements issue of *PW*, for example, runs to well over 400 pages; the spring announcements issue usually runs to about half that size, and the summer announcement pages, a fairly recent development, are even more limited. Juvenile book announcement issues appear only twice each year (spring and fall) and are much smaller in scope for obvious reasons.

Most publishing houses hold two seasonal sales conferences. The first is held in the spring to brief the sales reps on forthcoming titles and to provide them with catalogs and other materials they can take on sales calls to the many accounts in their territories. In the second sales conference, usually held early in December, the same process takes place for the house's spring titles.

The purpose of the sales conference is to give the sales reps enough information about each title selected for publication to enable them to sell the books to the bookseller, librarian, or institution. Regardless of this noble aim, the rep is still faced with the problem of selling something that as yet does not exist—a pig in a poke, as it were. One industry critic has described the publisher's rep as "essentially a Yankee peddler. . . . He comes rattling in with his horse and wagon, displays and extols the virtues of every pot and pan, knife, fork, and spoon, and odds and ends of tinware that he carries, and pleads with [the customer] to take some of each item" (Leonard Shatzkin, *In Cold Type: Overcoming the Book Crisis*, Houghton Mifflin, 1982).

The great difference, of course, is that even the Yankee peddler had actual forks and spoons to show; the book sales rep has nothing more than a little information, a catalog, and a lot of house hype to offer to the potential purchaser. It is hard to imagine another industry that not only has tens of thousands of unique products to sell each year, but also expects its buyers, for the most part, to accept them on faith.

Another problem for both reps and publisher is that the sales reps are expected to offer hundreds of titles to each potential customer. But since their livelihood depends on how many orders are placed, their natural tendency is to concentrate on those titles the customer is likely to buy in quantity. The lesser titles (only in the sense of salability) tend to be represented in a more desultory manner, if at all. As a result, advance orders on these books may be low, and—although advance orders are not necessarily an indication of a book's future sales—they are the main barometer by which publishers set print runs and marketing budgets.

RETURNS POLICY

The policy of returns is perhaps the most effective tool in the sales rep's bag of selling tricks, and yet it is the major problem in the book-distribution process. It allows the retail or wholesale customer to return any unsold books (or, in the case of paperbacks, only their covers!) within a year or so for full credit; the returner pays only return freight charges—a small price for overordering. In effect, publishers are offering their products to the customer on consignment—a practice followed in very few industries, if any, in this century. If a department store does not sell some items, for example, the store does not return them to the producer but puts them on sale for a reduced price, as do auto dealers and supermarkets.

Returns make it easy for the purchaser to order more books than may be really needed with very little direct risk. In 1984, Congdon & Weed—a good-sized and respected publishing house—folded, citing as one of the major reasons an inordinate and unexpected volume of returns. In early 1986, the giant Doubleday announced a 1985 loss of some $10 million, citing not enough best-sellers and too many returns as two of the major reasons for the loss. Von Holtzbrinck, the company mentioned above, asked the reader to consider that "33% of every shipment [of books] on average is returned for credit."

The problem of returns has plagued the publishing industry for decades, and its magnitude seems to increase in spite of widespread industry recognition of it deleterious effects. For the year 1998, returns accounted for 31.6 percent of trade sales—a drop of 5.1 percent from the previous year, but a substantial percentage nevertheless. In the mass-market paperback area, for every ten paperbacks sold, six will be returned—or their stripped covers (which has led to a lucrative black market for sales of stripped paperbacks—but that's another story). A former president of McGraw-Hill, Curtis Benjamin, stated in *Publishers Weekly* in 1981 that returns in 1979 cost the book business between $80 million and $120 million—a substantial percentage of the $4 billion in total sales for that year, but an estimate that many other experts in the industry say was far, far too low. The levels of returns have only increased as a percentage over the two decades since to the previously unheard of dollar level of more than $1.75 billion each year (*Publishers Weekly*, "High Flyers, Crash Landings," March 29, 1999, p. 28).

The returns policy, in addition to contributing to the sharply escalating annual cost for books, has a direct and deleterious effect on library book purchasing too—even though the percentage of books returned by libraries is nearly zero. It is a primary reason that so many books go out of print so quickly. No publisher, swamped with returns of unsold books, can afford to warehouse these books indefinitely, because the tax on warehouse inventory is murderous; it is much more economically sound to declare them out of print. As a result, there is probably no librarian in the country who has not at one time or another had the experience of selecting a book for purchase, verifying its availability in *Books in Print*, and placing an order for it, only to discover that it is not available either because it is out of stock (either for a given amount of time, but much more often "out of stock indefinitely") or completely out of print.

Not only do books go out of print all the time, but the rate increases yearly as well. For example, the new edition of Booksinprint.com 2000, Bowker's online version of *Books in Print*, features more than 160,000 new titles. It also notes that over the period between 1989 and 1999, nearly 175,000 titles went out of print, a stunning percentage. As industry critic Leonard Shatzkin pointed out, in his *In Cold Type: Overcoming the Book Crisis*, 90 to 95 percent of the trade books published in the United States each year are "stone cold dead by the end of their first year of life"—in other words, are out of print—and the life of the vast majority of paperbacks can be measured in weeks rather than months.

Why? The simplistic answer is that too many books are published each year, but the better answer is that too many books are unsold by the retailer and wholesaler each year and ultimately returned to the publisher. Why is this also a problem for library book purchasers? About half the books purchased by libraries in this country are trade books. However, only one-third of all trade books is sold to libraries; the other two-thirds are sold to wholesalers and retailers. But—and it's a big "but"—of those books sold to wholesalers and retailers, one out of every three will be returned to the publisher for full credit because it remained unsold for a few months to a year. And since the publisher cannot afford to warehouse and pay taxes on unsold merchandise indefinitely any more than any other producer of goods can, returned books are sold to remainder dealers for pennies on the dollar—or, in the case of those coverless paperbacks, are shredded and sold for waste paper. In both cases, when the inevitable happens, the books go out of print immediately. In simplest terms, the library market is not large enough to support trade publishing. The segment that *is* large enough to do it, the retail/wholesale market, is the segment that effectively determines which books will stay in print or not, all because of that antiquated, unwise, costly, and destructive part of the distribution process called "returns."

Is there an answer to this problem? Of course there is, and it's a simple one: print fewer copies of books and rescind returns policies, both of which will make tighter, more realistic inventory control a distinct possibility for publishers seeking to cut costs and stay in business. Is this likely to ever happen? Of course not. As the BISG/Andersen study reported and dozens of articles in trade and professional journals have reiterated over the years, returns policies are entrenched in the industry, and most publishers are loath to change them, no matter how costly they become.

Two things, then, should go without saying: trade publishing neither can nor will really come to terms with inventory control and reduction as long as half or more of their inventory may be in bookstores and wholesale warehouses waiting to be returned in three or six or twelve months; and libraries, which do *not* return books, will continue to pay more for them initially (since library discounts rarely equal those given to retailers and wholesalers), will continue to provide an indirect subsidy to those who do return books for credit, and will remain almost completely ineffective at influencing which titles stay in or go out of print.

OTHER PROBLEMS

The reader will recall that Joseph Deitch in his *Publishers Weekly* article "Moving Books Around" stated that publishing houses in 1982 were taking "a fresh look at what many regard as the industry's second most important function: getting books to customers at lower prices, more rapidly, and with less chance of damage." As far as lower prices go, just the opposite has happened: popular fiction has broken the $30 mark, few mass-market paperbacks can be had for less than $7.95, and nontrade publishing has matched or exceeded its trade counterparts in escalating prices at an enormous rate, much greater than the rate of inflation.

Books are not reaching their customers much faster than they did nearly two decades ago either. Since most publishers insist on shipping all but the largest orders via the U.S. Postal Service (USPS), it often takes more, not less, time to receive books—if one receives them at all. Too many publishers have yet to discover the joys of United Parcel Service (UPS) or Fedex or any of the other private delivery services. These companies are not only often cheaper than the USPS (particularly in light of the fact that smaller shipments are insured at no extra cost and larger ones cost less than the USPS charges), but also rarely lose, smash, soak, or smear grease and oil on parcels in the process of delivering them.

In short, the distribution process in the year 2000 is just about where it was and what it was more than fifty years ago. If O. H. Cheney were alive today, I have no doubt that he would still write exactly what he wrote a half century ago: that book distribution is "unsystematic, underdeveloped, ineffective, unprofitable, and static." *Plus ça change . . .*

5 WHY BOOKS COST WHAT THEY DO

There is probably not a librarian alive today who doesn't believe that the cost of books is much too high and has escalated much faster than that of many other manufactured objects. This belief is not the result of what some so-called authorities call their "lack of understanding of the book world"; rather, this belief has its basis in fact. One has only to compare the average prices of books listed in the *Bowker Annual* of the 1970s or 1980s with those quoted in a recent edition for proof that not only have books become extremely costly (and astronomically priced if you are in Canada) but also that the rate of increase in book prices has far surpassed the general rate of inflation. For example, the average price for a hardcover fiction book in 1972 was $6.47; by 1998 it had risen to $28.25. A juvenile hardcover that cost $4.37 in 1972 was priced at $16.12 by 1998. The average price for books on technology rose from $16.11 in 1972 to more than $85.00 in 1998, and the cost of a mass-market paperback increased from $1.12 to $9.31 over that same period. More simply put, the average cost of a book more than quadrupled in a quarter century, and still shows no sign of leveling off for the first decade of the new millennium.

It is not the purpose of this chapter to posit reasons for this increase in book prices over the years, however, but to explain what goes into determining those prices and why some categories of books are so much more costly than others. These are factors that librarians who purchase books can and should understand simply because they are basic to any understanding of the complexity of the economics of book publishing.

KINDS OF COSTS

Chapter 3 offered some indication of the financial risk involved in the decision to publish a book. Publishing is a highly risky business requiring a large outlay of capital long before the book is ready to be sold, sometimes even before the author has set the first word to paper. And this outlay of front money continues all through the editing, design, production, and marketing processes. The entire cost of producing books must be carefully predicted and constantly monitored so that the eventual price is enough to give publishers some return on their investment and thus enable them to stay in business—but not so high that customers will refuse to purchase the books. In short, publishing is a high-level balancing act worthy of the Flying Wallendas.

Although different authorities may use slightly different terminology in discussing the costs incurred in publishing a book, most agree that there are four broad factors that eventually determine what the cover price will be. These are overhead, royalties, sales costs, and production costs.

- *Overhead* is a fixed cost in any business; it can be defined as all the general costs of running the business other than costs for materials and production. Examples of a publisher's overhead are salaries and employee benefits, rent, office supplies and equipment, telephones and other communications equipment, postage, and interest on outstanding debts. As a fixed cost, overhead is integral to the cost of publishing a book and is a major factor in establishing a given book's final price.
- *Royalties* are a second major cost for the publisher. When a publisher signs a contract with an author, a stipulated percentage of the book's income is agreed upon as payment for the author. In many cases, particularly in trade publishing, a cash payment—called an advance against royalties or advance for short—is paid to the author upon signing a contract and before any writing has actually been done. For instance, suppose that author X contracts with publisher Y to write a book. Under the terms of the contract, X will be paid a $4,000 advance and royalties at 10 percent of the retail price of the book for the first 2,000 copies sold, 12.5 percent for the next 2,000 copies sold, and 15 percent for any additional copies sold. If the price of the book is $20, the author will earn $2.00 on each of the first 2,000 copies, $2.50 on the next 2,000, and $3 on copies sold thereafter. The author will not receive any royalty payments until sales exceed the 2,000 mark; $2 per book x 2,000 copies = $4,000, the amount of the advance against royalty. An author who fails to produce an acceptable manuscript—or a manuscript period—usually is obligated to return the advance to the publisher. Royalties, then, are a variable cost in publishing because the amount paid is determined by the number of copies sold.
- *Sales/Marketing costs* usually consist of commissions, catalogs, advertising and marketing, exhibit fees, travel, and other such expenses.
- *Production costs* make up the final cost area for the publisher. They include all the costs of producing a finished book from an author's manuscript. Part of this production cost is fixed or predictable, part is dependent on the number of units produced. The fixed cost of production is usually referred to as plant costs, which include such things as composition (typesetting or its more

modern equivalents), design and artwork, copyediting, proofreading, illustration, and color separations. Plant costs are onetime costs; once the book is designed, it is designed; once type is set, it's set; and so on, no matter how many times the book may go back for reprinting. Other production costs are not fixed costs, but are variable costs.

VARIABLE COSTS

The variable costs involved in production are usually referred to as manufacturing or running costs and encompass expenses such as paper, printing, and binding. They are variable because they depend on the number of copies of the book that are ultimately printed. It is selfevident that it takes more paper, more ink, and more binding material, as well as more labor and time running costly machinery, to produce 10,000 books than it does to produce 1,000 copies.

The publisher can be fairly sure of fixed costs such as overhead and plant costs. But since variable costs are not so easily predicted, certain other decisions must be made before arriving at a book's price. These decisions include such things as the kind of paper that will be used; cover materials; the type of binding the book will have; whether or not to use color besides black; and, ultimately, the number of copies in the first print run.

All of these decisions affect not only the cost of producing a book but also how it will look. However, appearance is not a major factor to all publishers. For example, publishers like Viking, Knopf, and Farrar, Straus & Giroux generally produce handsome books printed on high-quality paper, whereas other major trade publishers have books with sleazy covers that appear to be printed on paper that has been (badly) recycled out of old newspapers. (The latter publishers also tend to use poor-quality glue in their bindings, which gives rise to librarians' well-founded lament that "the book fell apart after two circulations!")

A good production supervisor not only will choose the most appropriate paper but also will buy as much of that paper as possible at one time to use for other books on the publisher's list in order to realize substantial cost savings. A number of other factors come into play here, however. If the book needs color photographs or other illustrations, the paper chosen must have a glossy finish, and glossy paper costs more than the paper used for nonillustrated fiction books, which are usually printed on rough or antique-finish paper.

The color of the paper itself is a factor; "white" paper ranges from pure, brilliant white to a yellowish or muddy gray tone; the higher the whiteness rating, the more costly the paper. Weight is another consideration: a 700–page fiction saga will of necessity be printed on a less bulky paper than a slim volume of poetry, for example. Finally, an important question to librarians especially is whether the paper is acid-free. Acid-free paper will last for many years without yellowing or crumbling, but it is also relatively expensive.

There are two general types of binding that hold the book's pages together: *sewn*, or edition binding and *perfect* binding, or binding that uses glue rather than sewing to hold the pages together. Sewn binding is very sturdy; it is also very expensive compared to perfect binding. One form of sewn binding, called Smyth sewn, allows a book to open flat; another form, side sewn, does not. Both are superior to perfect binding, however, which was once used only for paperbacks and other inexpensive books, but is now used by many publishers for general hardcovers. (These are the books mentioned above in which pages or sometimes whole signatures fall out after a circulation or two.)

Once the pages are bound, covers are attached to protect the pages to allow the book to stand upright on a shelf and to add to the aesthetic quality of the book. The cover's base is usually heavy cardboard (called binder's board) covered with cloth, paper, a combination of the two, or a plastic coating. Cloth is certainly the most attractive and most durable, but it costs more than paper or coated plastic. (A few publishers over the years have experimented with replacing binder's board with a heavy gauge, printed plastic cover, but for some reason this never caught on.)

A number of factors affect the critical decision of how many copies should be printed:

1. Is the author well known enough to sell a lot of copies on the strength of his or her name alone?
2. Is the book's topic of general or timely interest, or of limited interest?
3. Is the book likely to sell enough copies upon publication to earn an immediate profit, or is it more likely to become a backlist title and thus take a longer time to establish an acceptable profit?
4. How will the book be promoted and marketed?
5. Have any subsidiary rights been sold, especially to movies and television, book clubs, and paperback houses?

SAMPLE SCENARIO

To see how it all works, let's imagine what happens in a typical (but imaginary) publishing house.

Simon Simple, the owner of Simple Publishing Company, has a manuscript for a novel that he believes will make a salable book. Its author has had several other titles published by Simple Publishing, all

	Per Copy	Total 10,000 Copies	Total 5,000 Copies
Table 5.1 **Profit (Loss) Table**			
Revenue at 48% discount	$9.85	$98,500	$49,250
Less overhead of 40%	($3.94)	($39,400)	($39,400)
	$5.91	$59,100	$9,850
Less production cost	($3.10)	($31,000)	($22,500)
	$2.81	$28,100	$(12,650)
Less royalty	($1.89)	($18,900)	($9,450)
	$ .92	$9,200	$(22,100)

of which sold respectably, if not spectacularly—from 6,000 to 8,000 copies each. Mr. Simple believes that with a little extra push from the promotion and marketing people, this new novel, *The French Wench*, should be able to sell at least 10,000 copies. Not only does the author have a loyal following—her novels offer just enough titillation to keep readers coming back for more—but also two of her earlier novels sold for modest amounts to paperback reprint houses. The editorial staff agrees, so the production supervisor is asked to come up with an estimate of plant and manufacturing costs.

Simple's Profit (Loss) on *The French Wench*

With this information at hand, it is possible to project how well or how poorly Simple Publishing will do on *The French Wench*. If the publisher sells all 10,000 copies, or sells only half that number, the profit/loss picture will look something like that in Table 5.1.

If 10,000 copies sell, Simple Publishing will realize a profit of $9,200, plus half of whatever accrues from the paperback reprint contractual agreement (the other half going to the author) made with another publisher. If a fickle public decrees that the book isn't so great after all and buys only 5,000 copies, Simple will go in the hole for about $22,000, less whatever reprint rights bring in. The risky nature of the book-publishing business becomes clear from this example when one considers how many more profitable titles will have to be published by Simple Publishing to make up for just this one loser.

OTHER PRICING CONSIDERATIONS

There are several other factors that may affect the cover price of a book: the use of color for photography, art, charts, maps, or graphs. A thirty-two-page children's picture book with four-color illustrations, for example, may cost out as high as *The French Wench*. Another is the nature of the book itself. A thick, authoritative, general reference book may require a number of authors, all of whom have to be paid, plus the work of a number of editors who specialize in this kind of book. One good example of this is a general encyclopedia, and another is reference books such as Gale's *Contemporary Authors* series, which uses the services of dozens of editors. Overhead, and thus unit cost, are greater at Gale than at a trade house where half a dozen editors can handle dozens of books, so the higher prices for such reference materials are not really excessive.

Finally, there is the audience for whom the book is intended. A specialized scientific monograph may sell to only a few hundred readers worldwide, so its initial print run will reflect this. But this small print run will increase the cover price greatly, because the *fixed* costs involved in producing a book that will sell 300 copies are not that much less than those for producing a book whose profits will come from sales of 100,000 copies; the variable costs, however, are much, much lower.

THE PUBLISHER'S DILEMMA

After all is said and done, publishers only have a few choices if they are to increase their profits and minimize their losses. They can cut fixed costs such as overhead by laying off staff, but too much cost-cutting may lead to them acquiring, editing, and designing fewer titles and potentially losing part of their share of the market. A publisher can cut manufacturing costs by using less expensive paper and bindings and hiring production out to a less expensive printing company, but such cost-cutting too often leads to books of inferior quality. Finally, a publisher can raise revenue by increasing the book's cover price, but there are limits to how much even the most gullible book buyer will pay for a book, and increasing revenue in this way may decrease sales enough to negate projected profits.

In most cases, publishers probably do try to keep costs down and increase revenue by raising prices only when it is necessary. But once one publisher breaks a commonly accepted price barrier, too many others will follow, whether it's necessary or not. No acquisitions librarian ever thought a piece of pop fiction would exceed $30.00 in price, but that is now common. No one ever thought a mass-market paperback priced at more than $2.95 would sell, but prices of $6.95 to $9.95 are the norm today. And children's librarians probably never envisioned shelling out $21.00 for a picture book, but they are doing just that.

All of this creates a big problem for librarians, whose budgets, by and large, have not and likely never will keep pace with the spectacular increase in book prices. Where it will all end no one knows, but in the meantime we pay and pay, and pay some more—because we have no choice. This is all the more reason for us to keep book costs down in the only way we can, by choosing the best possible vendors, which is the subject of Chapters 7 and 8. But first let's look at some of the trends in publishing that also affect book costs.

6 SOME TRENDS IN BOOK PUBLISHING

In the mid-1970s, a group of California librarians began publishing an alternative journal called *Booklegger* for their colleagues who were not satisfied with the then-current crop of library publications. At that time, library journals best promoted conservative views of the library world and the issues facing those working in libraries, but they were also downright timid—some might say cowardly—when it came to discussing the more controversial trends and radical movements within the profession of librarianship, and those changes in the book-publishing industry that directly or indirectly affected librarians. Celeste West, one of *Booklegger*'s founders, was particularly concerned with the ever-increasing number of mergers and acquisitions within the publishing industry and their effects on the kinds and quality of books being published. In 1975, West predicted that as the number of trade publishers decreased through merger or acquisition, many fine publishing houses would disappear and that consequently library collections would suffer.

The accuracy of West's predictions was confirmed by the industry over the next two dozen years. By the year 2000, hardly a single major trade publisher (and few minor ones) had escaped merger or acquisition, the latter sometimes hostile. One by one, the great old publishing houses were acquired by other publishers or by conglomerates with little or no connection to the book-publishing business. One of the first of these was Simon & Schuster's acquisition in 1975 by Gulf & Western Industries, Inc. (now Paramount Communications), a company that owned Columbia Pictures and was only at the beginning of a veritable tidal wave of takeovers and mergers. Following the dissolution of other long-established houses, by the late 1970s several antitrust suits were brought by the U.S. Department of Justice, many of which remained in litigation for a decade or longer.

Over the next fifteen years some of the major acquisitions and takeovers were those of G. P. Putnam's Sons, taken over without a struggle by the gigantic entertainment conglomerate MCA, Inc.; then there was Atheneum's merger with Scribner's in 1979, and Scribner's subsequent takeover by Macmillan in 1984. Dodd, Mead became a subsidiary of a religious publishing house, Thomas Nelson, which was subsequently itself bought by a trio of entrepreneurs and soon found itself in financial difficulty, but Nelson soon recovered and by 1995 was the ninth largest trade publisher in the United States, even with its output limited to religious books. Lippincott was taken over by Harper & Row, which was itself acquired by newspaper czar Rupert Murdoch's News

Corporation in 1987 and reborn as HarperCollins. Doubleday acquired mass-market paperback publishers Dell Books, Delacorte Press, and Dial Press; then was itself acquired, along with Bantam Books, by Bertelsmann AG, a giant German publishing firm.

Prentice-Hall was purchased by Gulf & Western in 1984 and became a subsidiary of that company's Simon & Schuster, making S & S the largest trade publisher in the nation at that time. But S & S did not remain at that pinnacle for long, however; by 1998, Random House, owned by the newspaper family, Newhouse, had purchased Times Books and Crown Publishers, making Random the country's largest trade publisher. Viking Press was bought by the British house, Penguin, which later, as the Penguin Group, acquired Dutton, Putnam Berkley, G. P. Putnam's, and a host of other hardcover and paperback publishers. The Time Warner conglomerate bought Warner Books, Little, Brown, Time-Life Books, and others, while another German publishing company, Holtzbrinck, was acquiring Farrar, Straus & Giroux, Henry Holt, and St. Martin's Press, among others. There were many other moves of this type throughout the1980s and 1990s, culminating in Bertelsmann's acquisition of Random House and all its holdings from the Newhouse family in 1998, which then made the Bertelsmann group the largest publishing conglomerate in America.

At the time of this writing, the number of major American trade publishers who had *not* been acquired or taken over was in the single digits. But the phenomenon was not limited to adult trade houses. Children's book publishers, educational publishers, paperback (both mass market and quality) houses, technical/professional publishers—everyone was fair game, and few were the houses that escaped unscathed. The brief roster of changes above gives only some indication of the turmoil that has beset the book-publishing industry during recent years, and it shows no sign of subsiding even now.

How have these rapid and revolutionary changes in the book-publishing business affected the acquisition of books for library collections? There are a number of answers, not many of which are encouraging, and they arise from the impetus behind the mania to merge that has characterized book publishing over the last few decades. The chief reason, as one might guess, is economics, the same reason for the major upheavals among many other American industries in the 1980s and 1990s. As has been noted earlier, publishing has always been a risky business and, for most publishers, one where profits are modest compared to those of other industries. Book publishing is also a very small industry in comparison with, say, automobile manufacturing or the oil industry; many individual American companies have gross annual sales that exceed those of the entire book-publishing industry. Why then are such giant conglomerates as Paramount Communications (formerly Gulf & Western), Viacom, and Time

Warner interested in acquiring such relatively modest operations as publishing companies?

There are a number of good financial reasons. For one, while publishing is a high-risk business that requires a substantial investment long before the finished book is ready to be sold, the rewards—if the book is a big seller—can be substantial; the profit to be gained from having one or more authors who can write the "big number" books can be enormous and help write off all the publisher's other mistakes in judgment. For example, *Publishers Weekly*, in the December 14, 1998 issue, did a lengthy profile of one of the kind of authors every publisher hopes to find. Dean Koontz is perhaps not a megawriter like Tom Clancy or Danielle Steel or John Grisham, but his sales figures are astonishing. According to *PW*, Koontz has been writing for about thirty years and has had published "nearly 80 books with aggregate sales of more than 200 million units worldwide in 33 countries. Each year, [his] frontlist and backlist combined sell about 17 million copies worldwide." Just to get an idea of how much one new Koontz book can be worth to his publisher, Bantam Books, let's look at what happened to *Fear Nothing*, published in January 1998. The book's cover price was $26.95 per copy. The first printing was 400,000 copies, with a total cover price value of $10,780,000. The discount the publisher had to offer to wholesalers and retailers was probably around 50 percent, which left Bantam Books with about $5,390,000 to play with. Of the 400,000 copy first printing, all were sold. The author's royalties (15 percent of the original cover price) approximated $1,616,000, while production costs came to about $2,156,000; the two major costs, then, add up to about $3,772,000, leaving Bantam with a gross of approximately $1,618,000—not exactly peanuts. When a few other things are factored in, the profit really begins to grow. Almost immediately after its original publication date, Bantam had a second print run of another 100,000 copies; the profit on these would be greater because the only costs for the additional copies would be the variable costs, such as paper, binding, and printing. In addition, large-print rights were sold, and a limited, signed edition ($150 per copy) was printed. And since Bantam is also in the paperback business and had the rights to reprint in that format, the costs for Bantam were less to produce the paperback edition itself. (In December 1998, Bantam shipped its first paperback printing of *Fear Nothing*, 1.8 million copies, to tie in with publication of Koontz's new book, *Seize the Night*, also scheduled for December 1998 publication, with a first run of 400,000 copies.)

Even when a publishing house does not have a spectacularly successful writer such as a Dean Koontz or a Stephen King (who was reported by the British paper *The Guardian* in February 2000 to have signed a three-book contract with his British and American publishers—Hodder and Stoughton and Simon & Schuster, respectively—for $48 million) on its roster, however, good editorial staff who know how to choose books with sales potential can go far toward ensuring profits that are steady, even if relatively modest, over a long period of time. One example is St. Martin's Press, long an independent publisher but now owned by the German Holtzbrinck organization. St. Martin's rarely publishes a "blockbuster" title but instead produces some 600 solid titles each year that are bought primarily by libraries—including mysteries, regency fiction, science fiction, and gay fiction—to produce a return on investment of more than 30 percent, a very respectable return in any investor's language. And in early February of 1999, the *New York Times* carried the obituary of publisher Marion Boyars, who published "only what she liked, whether the book was likely to sell or not"; and although the names of most of the authors of the 500 titles she published may be unfamiliar to most American readers, among them were dozens of the world's finest writers, including four Nobel Prize for Literature winners and a number of other prestigious award winners.

Another source of relatively modest but steady profit can be a house's children's line; practically no one but libraries purchases hardcover children's books, but they purchase them in quantity and over the years. Wanda Gag's *Millions of Cats*, for example, has been in print for nearly half a century, but every year hundreds of libraries purchase new copies because the little book is beloved by children, and the copies simply wear out from being read and handled so much. HarperCollins, perhaps one of the biggest and most successful publishers of children's books, attributes a great deal of its financial success over the years to its juvenile line. This kind of slow but constant return on investment over the long haul is very attractive to investors—as HarperCollins proved to be to Rupert Murdoch's News Corporation.

At the same time, the very smallness of the publishing world makes it attractive to investors. A conglomerate seeking to diversify might have to spend tens of billions to take over a major company in, say, automobile manufacturing or pharmaceuticals. In 1984, however, Gulf & Western paid some $700 million in its takeover bid for what was then the largest American publisher, Prentice-Hall; this sum was far, far less than what it would have had to pay for Ford Motor Company or General Motors; it was only in the late 1990s that a few book-publishing company buyouts exceeded a billion dollars. To the investor seeking to diversify holdings without assuming major financial obligations, a publishing house can be a real bargain.

For librarians, the ongoing concentration of the publishing industry caused by mergers and acquisitions has both positive and negative aspects. On the positive side, it has on occasion resulted in saving some publishing houses from going under because of financial pressures, which for libraries means that a certain degree of diversity in the publishing of the books we choose to buy is maintained. A good example is that of Atheneum, a distinguished house created in 1958 by three of the best men in the book business—Alfred Knopf, Jr., Simon Michael Bessie, and Hiram Hayden. It was, said the *New York Times* on March 15, 1958, "as if the presidents of General Motors, Chrysler, and Ford left their jobs to start a new automobile company." The books they published not only were distinguished literarily but also sold well. However, a lack of capital—as well as personality conflicts among the partners—brought the fledgling company to the point of financial crisis by the 1970s. The owners realized that an infusion of much-needed capital could only come from sale of the company or from merging with another publisher.

The one thing they agreed on was that they did not want to be taken over by a nonbook corporation that would swallow them up, and so they refused any such offers. The solution came, however, in Atheneum's merger with Scribner's. As a result, Atheneum was able to continue to produce a line of critically praised books through the next few decades—even after 1984, when Scribner's merged with Macmillan (which was itself bought by Maxwell Communications). Doubleday, too, faced a major financial crisis during the 1970s and was finally bailed out by Bantam, later of course itself acquired by Bertelsmann. In both cases, the alternative to merger appeared to be oblivion, and these are not isolated or even uncommon cases.

There is another side to that positive aspect mentioned above, however. For every publishing house that has been saved, another has been lost through acquisition or takeover. As discussed earlier, Doubleday bought one of trade publishing's most prestigious lines when it acquired Dial Press, only to dissolve the newly acquired company a short time later because of the parent company's financial difficulties. Coward-McCann, another fine house, was bought by Putnam's, and then quickly disappeared from the publishing scene entirely. World Publishing, once a giant in the industry, was taken over by New American Library in the late 1960s and within a few years just faded away; ironically, NAL's new owner, Penguin, soon abandoned New American Library to the same fate. Juvenile publishing was not immune to the wave of the 1970s and 1980s, either. A fine children's house, Bradbury Press, was bought by Macmillan, probably because of that house's stellar author Judy Blume, but soon after Bradbury was allowed to wither on the vine. In the late 1990s, two more excellent lines were lost too; Cobblehill and Lodestar Books each counted a number of prizewinners among their authors but still bit the dust.

By the end of the 1990s, dozens of the grand old names in publishing no longer existed, and library collections could only be the worse for the loss, because every company's demise lessens a library's purchasing options. But add to this another development of the last few decades, the rise of the "blockbuster" book, and the negative effect of publishing trends on library collections becomes even more obvious.

More than a decade ago, Joni Evans, then president of Simon & Schuster's trade division, said in an address to the American Booksellers Association convention, "It's a dramatic and sexy time now [for publishers]; it feels like we're the new Hollywood." She was referring to the then-new (but still flourishing) emphasis in trade publishing on the blockbuster book, a book that can be expected to sell hundreds of thousands or even millions of hardcover copies at an extraordinarily rapid rate. Books by Stephen King, Danielle Steel, John Grisham, and a few others can almost guarantee this kind of sale and so guarantee whopping profits for their publishers. Evans went on to say that she'd rather pay $2 million to one author like this for a new book than buy ten lesser (in the sense of sales) authors' works at a tenth of that cost each, primarily because with big-name authors the risk is just not there.

What this kind of thinking portends for library book purchasers is obvious. Librarians, especially in public libraries, do buy best-sellers, but good librarians are likely to be just as interested in obtaining the works of those ten "lesser" authors that Evans would prefer not to publish at all. Publishing's response to criticism of this sort is to say that it's the blockbuster books that make it possible to publish the works that won't sell in huge quantities; at one time, Doubleday published a small but influential line of poetry books and claimed that it was the "biggies" that paid for its poetry's continuing existence (which shortly after met a quiet demise), but there's little real evidence that this relationship of best-sellers and less than "best"-sellers has any real connection. At the same time, paying millions of dollars up front for a certain author's new book means that the publisher must recoup that amount and do it quickly; the easiest way to do so is to charge more for the finished book, and there's little doubt that this is a major factor in the continuing escalation of book prices—a very real concern for libraries. (It is interesting to read *Publishers Weekly*'s annual issues in which they describe publishers' would-be best-sellers that turned out instead to be bombs. The stories would be amusing if it weren't for the ugly fact that library dollars did a lot to pick up those losses.)

The impact of higher prices on libraries is that libraries can purchase fewer and fewer books each year—even when library budgets show a modest increase. In fact, very few librarians saw their budgets increase by 100 percent or more in the 1980s and 1990s, yet book prices tripled during that period. In addition, the nothing-short-of-phenomenal increases in serials' prices over the last decade, plus the increasing pressure on libraries to spend more on electronic information sources, have also had a profound effect on library book purchasing. Ergo, for reasons completely beyond their control, librarians are buying fewer books, and fewer books mean weaker collections. No one expects that publishers will help the situation by ceasing to risk so much to get these phenomenally salable books, but while "blockbuster" may mean "sexy" to Joni Evans and publishers like hers, there's nothing sexy about them at all; there *is* something just plain greedy about the whole situation, however.

PART II

THE BOOK
ACQUISITIONS PROCESS

7 VENDORS: RETAILERS AND PUBLISHERS

> The more you know about the economics of those you
> buy from, the more effectively you can deal with them.
> Daniel Melcher,
> *Melcher on Acquisition*

On the face of it, the librarian has only three choices when it comes to choosing vendors to supply books: Books can be purchased directly from their producer, the publisher; from the wholesalers whose function it is to buy books from publishers and resell them to libraries and retail booksellers; or from retail booksellers themselves, either from stores or from a number of retailers who sell their wares via the Internet. The decision as to which vendor or vendors to use is not a simple one, however.

There are literally thousands of publishers in the United States, dozens of wholesalers, and countless retail booksellers in nearly every city and town; most of these purveyors of books are anxious to sell them to libraries. Each entity has its own policies for dealing with the library market, and each has certain strengths and weaknesses. Knowledge of these elements is the best way to guarantee what every library book-buyer seeks: the best possible service at the best possible price.

But how does one gain this necessary knowledge? Trial and error is hardly the answer; it simply doesn't work because of the large number of variables involved. As a result, the librarian who is not aware of these variables and how to use them to greatest advantage will find the process of choosing a vendor an exercise in frustration—not only for the librarian, but ultimately for the library's patrons, who get peeved when the books they seek either do not appear on the shelves at all, or eventually appear only months after interest in them has peaked. Lack of knowledge can also be very costly; some vendors may take advantage of the unprepared librarian's naiveté and resort to less than ethical tactics once they have the library's business, perhaps inflating prices arbitrarily, playing with discounts, or the like. Simply accepting vendors' claims concerning discount and order fulfillment as the final and ultimate truth isn't very smart either. Any vendor representative with minimal corporate intelligence will promise every one of his or her prospective customers the sun, the moon, and the stars—all at the highest discounts in the business. The problem is that this just isn't going to happen, no matter how good the vendor is.

The only way to make wise decisions regarding book suppliers is to find out all you can about each type of vendor and then ask two basic questions of others who have had experience with a number of vendors: first, which ones they use and why; and second, which ones should be avoided and why. The first step mentioned above is the easy one; you can begin by asking specific questions of the publishers' or wholesalers' representatives, or by writing or calling someone at the company. Keep in mind, however, that when you do this, you'll be highly unlikely to hear much about the negative side of the vendors' services. An even better tactic is to make a few phone calls to large library systems, which will usually get you somewhat more objective information. Meetings and conferences also are fertile sources of information. Talk to your colleagues and find out who really is fair, honest, and efficient, and who isn't. A small investment of time and effort can give the astute acquisitions librarian a real edge in what is too often a cutthroat business.

PUBLISHERS AS VENDORS

With a few exceptions, it is possible to purchase just about any book in print from its publisher, and there are often good reasons for going directly to the source. In the first place, if the book is still in print, the publisher is more likely than anyone else to have copies available for sale. At the same time, if the book is unavailable for whatever reason, the publisher will report this, often more accurately than wholesalers do.

Some of the order-status information that is routinely given by reputable publishers in their status reports includes:

- *OP*. The title is *out of print*. There is no point in trying to order it from this publisher or from a wholesaler.
- *OS*. The title is *out of stock* at this time but will sooner or later be reprinted. If a reprint date is set, the publisher will report that date also.
- *OSI*. The title is *out of stock indefinitely*. This simply means that the publisher isn't willing to let the title go out of print yet, but hasn't decided to reprint it either.
- *NYP*. The title is *not yet published* but is scheduled for publication. If there is a firm pub date, this will be reported here.
- *NOP*. *Not our publication*. For some reason the order was sent to the wrong publisher. Do a little verification and send it to the correct publisher.

With most publishers, you will get most of what you order; however, items not shipped will be those reported using one of the above codes. (There are a few other codes, but they are rarely used and need no consideration here.)

Items that are not shipped (except OP titles) are usually *back ordered*; that is, the order is held open by the publisher until the books become available or until the end of the period of time that the library has stipulated as its limit (cancellation period). The stipulated back-order period can be any length the librarian wishes, but ninety days seems to be the most common and the most workable. It does not tie up the library's funds interminably, yet it gives the publisher a reasonable chance to reprint or to reach publication date within the specified period. If back-ordered titles are not available for shipment within the time frame, they are reported as canceled to the ordering library, which then has the choice of reordering the same book or spending its money on another title.

So far, so good. The library orders; then the publisher ships materials available and reports accurately on unavailable materials. Those publishers (or their order-fulfillment agencies) who are good at it fill orders fast and accurately, report promptly, supply accurate invoices, ship in containers strong enough to protect their contents from damage, use reputable and cost-efficient shipping companies, give the library a reasonable discount, and make the process of returning books and receiving credit for them (usually few or none) as simple and as efficient as possible. It soon becomes obvious to the library book purchaser which publishers are not responsible, and obtaining those publishers' products from a wholesaler instead is the best way of circumventing some publishers' sloppy and inefficient distribution practices.

Ordering from the publisher can be especially valuable to librarians who want some or all of the books in a hurry, but again, this all depends on how good the publisher's distribution system is. Most publishers can't hold a candle to certain of the big wholesalers, whose online ordering capacity almost guarantees delivery of materials in stock, in their warehouses within a day or two. The catch, of course, is the *in stock* part; if a book is not in the wholesaler's warehouse at the time a library orders it, the wholesaler first has to order it and then fill the library's order, thereby adding some delay to the fulfillment process. For this reason, many public librarians who like to have "hot" titles such as probable best-sellers or books on timely topics on the shelves as quickly as they are available in bookstores see ordering directly from the publisher as a real benefit, since it is a recognized fact that the bigger the book, in the case of best-sellers, the quicker the reading public wants it. Once interest peaks, however—usually within a month or two of its hardcover publication, but always once the paperback becomes available—demand diminishes. There is nothing quite so dead as a Danielle Steel or Tom Clancy novel in hardcover a year after its publication date.

Some librarians do not buy best-sellers but still require timely receipt of certain materials, such as reference books that are published on a regular, usually annual, basis. Suppose one orders a set of print encyclopedias at a cost of, say, $1,200. Prorating that over a year, the library is paying $100 each month for the set. If the sets are shipped four months into the year, however, those same books cost the library $150 per month. Similarly, every month that the library doesn't have the 2000 edition that it has ordered of *Metals Handbook* finds the value of the book reduced as well as its cost increased. The only ways to ensure timely receipt are to send orders directly to the publisher or to place such orders on a standing-order basis. In fact, it is necessary to do so for some materials; most encyclopedia publishers, for example, do not sell their wares to wholesalers for resale, and many reference-book publishers follow the same practice.

Whether it's a sure best-seller, a reference book, or a book that is likely to be in high demand for other reasons, it is wise to order the title six to eight weeks in advance of publication date. Many library systems, for example, order large quantities of a best-selling author's forthcoming title within this time frame because few publishing houses pay any attention to their announced publication dates; instead they ship books as soon as they are available from the printer—possibly weeks before the announced dates. As a result, these libraries have the books in-house as fast as the bookstores do; by giving this kind of book priority in cataloging and processing, it can be on the shelves and ready for patrons within a day or so of their receipt. This keeps both patrons and branch librarians happy, and it also gladdens the hearts of technical services staff when they no longer hear the eternal cry, "Where are our books?"

There is also a special reason for ordering reference books in advance of publication date. Most reference publishers print only a certain number of copies, based on the previous year's sales. There is little point in their printing enough copies "in case" there is greater demand—since experience has shown that demand remains fairly constant—or for purposes of backlist, since no one wants a warehouse full of backlist titles once the next years' editions have rendered them obsolete. In short, late ordering of this type of materials is likely to leave the library with no copies at all; the supply is used up and that's that. Just a little forethought can avoid this unpleasant scenario and maintain valuable materials in the library's collection.

There are some disadvantages to ordering directly from the publisher, however. Any librarian who orders a variety of books in substantial numbers recognizes that dealing direct means a multitude of shipments, an increase in shipping costs (almost always paid by the library), and many invoices to be processed and checks for payment issued. This adds up to an increase in both the possibility of error and a large investment of staff time and effort—that is, money. Plus, there are just too many publishers for the library to deal with them all on a direct basis. Even thinking of sending orders directly to the publisher for all the books that even a small or medium-sized library may want boggles the mind; for larger libraries it amounts to sheer madness. In addition, each publisher has its own policy for distributing books to libraries and charging for them, so too many direct orders can make it nearly impossible to anticipate elements such as the actual price the library will pay for the book, how it will be shipped, how well or how poorly the shipper will pack the books, what the invoice will look like, or how easy or how difficult it will be to return a damaged or wrong book for credit. In other words, monitoring vendor performance is a difficult job to begin with; keeping track of hundreds of dealers and thousands of transactions is nearly impossible.

Finally, libraries almost always pay substantially more for books ordered from a publisher than they do if books are ordered from a good wholesaler. Publishers, by and large, have a singular double standard in their dealings with libraries vis-à-vis wholesalers and retail booksellers. This is reflected nowhere more vividly than in an annual volume published by the American Booksellers Association, *The ABA Bookbuyers Handbook*. This fat volume lists the discount policies of nearly every major publisher in the United States. I use the plural intentionally, because just about every publisher listed in the *Handbook* presents *two* sets of discount policies: one for wholesalers/retailers and one for libraries/institutions. Almost without exception, the discounts for the latter group are substantially lower and in many cases nonexistent. In fact, book prices charged to libraries average 20 percent more than what booksellers pay for exactly the same items. Why?

In the first place, publishers have traditionally viewed the library market as a rather unimportant one. They tend to think of library dollars as relatively insignificant; of libraries as being notoriously slow payers of their bills; of library business practices as highly and needlessly complex and hopelessly out of date; of libraries purchasing only single copies of most books; of every sale to a library as an absolute guarantee that a reader somewhere will not buy a copy of the book if he or she can get a copy at the library "for nothing." Finally, there is the publisher's argument that libraries really only want to buy from wholesalers anyway, and, given a choice, will inevitably do so; why, then, cater to the library market?

Just how valid are these assertions? Not very. The "insignificance" of library dollars was indicated more than a decade ago when the Association of American Publishers, at its annual meeting in Rye, New York, called one segment of its program "Libraries: The Two Billion

Dollar Market" (that year's total annual book volume was $6 billion!). In the year 2000, that ratio remains close: nearly $8 billion for libraries out of about $26 billion annual volume, according to the *Bowker Annual*. And a hefty segment of those library billions includes a lot of books purchased that pretty much only libraries buy: first novels, poetry, overpriced reference sets, backlist and midlist titles, genre fiction hardcovers, hardcover juvenile books—the list goes on and on.

What about libraries being slow to pay their bills because of their "complex and archaic" business practices? To the former I answer that libraries are no worse than retailers and wholesalers in paying up, and probably a lot better. *Publishers Weekly* provides a great deal of page space, especially in its "Letters" section, to tales of booksellers having their credit cut off because of nonpayment of their bills, or of bookstores that have gone out of business for the same reason. Half-a-dozen major wholesalers have also gone belly up over the last three decades because their bills got so high that publishers cut off their credit. And what makes this particularly ironic is that both retailers and wholesalers are allowed to return any book unsold, for full credit, for up to a year after the book has sat on the shelves of the store or warehouse, yet they can't keep up with their book bills? Anyone with minimal common sense might ask the publishing community how a publisher can *ever* know the state of his or her business when at any time he or she may be inundated with returns for which the buyer will receive face value. A librarian might venture to say that the publishing industry's returns policy does not lend itself to good business practice, but after all, that's how publishers started selling books back in the eighteenth century. And libraries are archaic?

Indeed, it is also hard to conceive of a more complex and wasteful business practice than trying to maintain a dual accounting system, as publishers do routinely for booksellers on the one hand and libraries on the other. Consider that libraries do order a lot of single copies of books, but so do retail booksellers. (In fact, many libraries frequently order in multiples much larger than their retail counterparts, but that's easy to forget.) Publishers denigrate library single-copy orders but bend over backwards to support booksellers' single-copy orders with a process called STOP (Single Title Order Plan), by which booksellers, if they meet a few simple criteria, can get at least a 40 percent discount on each and every single-copy order. Libraries pay full price, with no discount for the same items and have never even had a STOP system offered to them. And, as any good independent booksellers will tell you, the individualized special ordering they do—almost always for a single copy of a book—is what keeps them in business, especially in the face of increasing competition from the chain bookstores.

And then there's that hoary old clinker that holds that somehow if a library buys a book to circulate "free," it means lower sales for publishers, since no reader will buy a book that is available for nothing. This bogus reasoning gives the publishing world another rationale for deprecating library sales even though it has about as much validity as leaving your molar under your pillow at night for the Tooth Fairy. The truth is that most library users are book people—people who need or want books enough to pay cash for them from time to time, even though the same books may be available in their nearby library. In addition, bookstore locations and sales seem to have no relation to the number and size of libraries in their immediate vicinity. Very often, in fact, communities with extensive library facilities have the largest number of bookstores. And, interestingly enough, each year bookstore sales rise at a rate of about 10 percent—almost exactly as much as library budgets rise each year. If libraries are buying more books, according to prevailing publishing wisdom, then bookstores and bookstore sales ought to be diminishing, which is patently not the case, nor has it ever been.

If nothing else indicates that books will continue to sell no matter how many libraries exist or how many books they have in their collections, the contemporary phenomenon of the chain bookstore does. There is scarcely a community in the country big enough to have even a small shopping mall that does not have its own Borders or Barnes & Noble bookstore; the chains continue to proliferate at an incredible rate. The fact that all these "bookstored" communities have libraries certainly hasn't stopped the growth of the chains and shows no indication of doing so, any more than libraries have ever had a harmful effect on bookstore sales. What the chains *are* facing in the new millennium, however, is a much more dangerous competitor than the local library, and that is the phenomenal growth of bookselling over the Internet by such companies as Amazon.com. Recognizing this real threat has caused some of the nation's largest chains, Barnes & Noble for one, to set up their own Websites and aggressively market over the Internet; where this will all end up is moot at this point, but it is already beginning to change the face of retail bookselling.

Finally, we have the argument that libraries traditionally buy books from wholesalers, not direct from publishers: there is a great deal of truth to this, but there are also good reasons for it. The first is that publishers, intentionally or otherwise, have done just about everything they can—such as the discriminatory discounting—to send library dollars into the coffers of the wholesaler. If anyone doubts that these discriminatory practices occurred, hark back to the U.S. Senate hearings in the 1960s, which ended with a number of publishers settling up with libraries to the tune of $11 million to avoid prosecution for price fixing; it's all there, in the public record. Given discriminatory pricing and discounting, as well as active discouraging by some publishers of direct library business, is it any wonder that libraries have traditionally bought the bulk of their books from wholesalers?

One can only conclude that many American publishers would like to see direct library sales just fade away, to be serviced totally by the wholesalers. This is unlikely, however, given the state of that industry at the dawn of the millennium and the controversies generated by some wholesalers when they *do* get all of some libraries' business. (A discussion of these and other problems in dealing with wholesalers follows in Chapter 8.) For good reason, libraries will continue to mix their sources for books and will continue to press for fairness in the pricing and discounting of those books to libraries. Is this likely to happen? It should be noted that many years ago the ALA Council, the ruling body of the American Library Association, passed a resolution that asked trade-book publishers to examine their individual discount policies in light of their fairness (or lack thereof) to library customers. Although there has been no action on the resolution taken by publishers since then, readers of this book are strongly urged to continue to press for fairer policies. It is in the interest of every library to do so.

BUYING FROM RETAILERS

A final word is in order on the use of retail booksellers as a source for library books. There may be occasions when this makes perfectly good sense for the library book purchaser—for instance, sudden insistent patron demand after an author appears on a major television talk show, or needing more copies immediately when requests for a very hot title begin to get out of hand. In many cases, local bookstores may specialize in books that are hard to locate or not easily available from traditional sources; examples may be a store that specializes in African American books or gay books. It may be easier and not much more costly to get the materials from such a local source—plus the local source may be a gold mine of ideas for titles that could be used in the collection but aren't reviewed in the usual journals.

In terms of good public relations for the library, these strategies may pay off, and so the extra cost of such books may well be worth it, but there definitely is a cost factor. A book that the library can get from a wholesaler or even some publishers at a 30 to 40 percent discount will rarely be discounted more than 10 or 20 percent by the retailer (except, of course, for titles that appear on the *New York Times* bestseller list, which are usually discounted by 30 percent or more), and it is unfair to ask for more than that. The retailer certainly cannot sell books for what he/she pays for them or the store will not be in business for long, so a smaller discount is not unreasonable. At the same time, titles that are in high demand in the library are often in high demand at retail stores; many retailers resist selling their stock of high-demand titles to libraries at a discount when they can sell to their regular customers at full price, and rightfully so. Add to that the fact that if the store sells too much of this inventory to libraries and doesn't have books left to sell to retail customers, those customers may be lost forever.

The retail bookseller is a good source only for very special purchases or when time is of the essence. Occasional and careful use of this source can be valuable for the library book buyer, and the benefits may sometimes far outweigh the additional dollars spent, but the caveats above should be considered before using this source routinely.

8 VENDORS: WHOLESALERS

> If one is to buy books effectively, there is no substitute for a good working knowledge of the economics of wholesaling.
>
> Daniel Melcher,
> *Melcher on Acquisition*

Few purchasers of books for libraries would question the fact that doing the bulk of one's ordering from a wholesaler or wholesalers is, for the most part, a wise policy. Faced with some publishers' reluctance or even outright refusal to sell their books directly to libraries, along with their poor service to and discriminatory pricing/discounting practices for their library customers, the acquisitions librarian is, in many instances, virtually forced to use the services of wholesalers. And it is certainly true that combining orders for many separate titles of disparate publishing houses can be both cost and time efficient; it is a lot easier to handle one shipment of 200 books with a single invoice than to cope with 200 books in, say, 20 shipments, each with its own invoice—and postage and shipping costs that will certainly surpass that for one shipment. It is also easier to monitor the performance of one or two or even a dozen wholesalers than hundreds or even thousands of individual publishers.

Many wholesalers offer services to their library customers that publishers are unable or unwilling to provide. These include free or inexpensive catalog cards (although with the advent of online catalogs this is less of a selling point than in the past); fully processed books or book-processing kits; approval, standing-order, and book-leasing plans; access to timely (usually updated weekly) microfiche or online information on activities in the book world that may influence a librarian's purchasing decisions; access to in-print book information that is often more up-to-date and thus more useful than that found in the print or online version of *Books in Print*; and finally (and increasingly), online access to wholesalers' databases, including the most important information for the acquisitions librarian, warehouse inventory, about which more will be said later in this chapter.

It would seem, then, that ordering books from wholesalers is not only a good idea but also the answer to the acquisitions librarian's prayers. But it isn't that simple, of course. A great deal of care must be taken in the selection of these vendors, and equal effort must be spent in monitoring all aspects of their service performance as long as they remain vendors of choice; if the library's standards are not maintained, then the only choice is to "de-select" the poor performer and start all over with someone else. Like any other business, book wholesaling has its pros and cons, which arise from the radically changed and changing nature of the wholesaling business itself and also from the volatile nature of the publishing industry. There is intense competition among wholesalers for library dollars, and some indulge in sleazy practices to get library customers and to increase their profit margins in this dog-eat-dog business.

CHOOSING WHOLESALERS

There are two broad categories of book wholesalers from which the librarian can choose. First there are *full-line wholesalers*, which stock a broad variety of titles from a large number of publishers: trade books, paperbacks, juvenile books, art books, small-press titles, remainders, university-press titles, technical and professional books, audio books, and so on. These wholesalers usually maintain good-sized inventories of new titles as well as those backlist titles that are important to their library customers.

A major wholesaler such as Ingram Books or Baker & Taylor will stock 70,000 or more titles in their several distribution centers and, if a title is not in stock, will be happy to order the book for the library customer if it is still available. Theoretically, it is possible for a library book purchaser to obtain the vast majority of titles needed from just one such wholesaler. In practice, however, this may not be such a good idea, for reasons discussed later in this chapter.

The second type of wholesaler is the *specialized wholesaler*, which stocks titles only within a certain category or categories. An example of this is Book Wholesalers Inc., which stocks only children's books; another is Quality Books, which warehouses small-press titles almost exclusively. This is not to say that most specialized wholesalers will turn away an order for a book that does not fall within their specialties, but only that they *stock* special categories of books. All but a few specialized wholesalers will order just about anything their customers want, just as full-line wholesalers will.

Whatever the type of wholesaler they choose, librarians generally should expect the following:

- a large inventory of titles in stock
- prompt order fulfillment
- accurate order fulfillment

- accurate order-status reporting
- reasonable and competitive discounts
- strict adherence to each library's policies regarding invoicing, cancellation of titles, returns, claims and exchanges, backordering, batching of shipments, and the like
- services such as online ordering, catalog cards, processed books or processing kits, approval or standing-order plans

LARGE TITLE INVENTORY

The primary reason a librarian uses wholesalers is precisely for their inventory. If the librarian is, so to speak, going to put all or most of the library's eggs (dollars) in one basket, then the basket had better be a good-sized one. Ideally, any wholesaler should maintain an inventory that includes a substantial percentage of those titles that fall within its purview. Grandiose claims to the contrary, even the largest wholesalers cannot possibly stock all titles published within most categories, given the fact that more than 60,000 new titles are published each year and that approximately 1.9 million titles are in print in any given year. In actuality, according to the Book Industry Study Group, only about 20 percent of current in-print titles account for 80 percent of most wholesalers' sales volume, so a stock of the *proper* 20 percent—one that will best meet the needs of its library customers—is what makes a wholesaler good enough to stay in business.

Two caveats are in order here, though. First, the librarian must be very leery of any wholesale book dealer who claims to be able to provide "any book in print," or "any book published in the United States," or even, as one vendor claims to be able to do, to obtain "any book published in the English language." Such claims are arrogant nonsense; no wholesaler can do this simply because some publishers, such as most encyclopedia publishers and publishers of certain major reference works, don't allow their books to be distributed by wholesalers. It is far more important for the wholesaler to be honest enough to let the library customer know which publishers' products it can or cannot supply so that the customer is not continually wasting time and money sending orders to the wholesaler only to have them unfilled. Certain of the larger wholesalers will, on request, supply the library with regularly updated lists of the publishers whose wares they *cannot* supply; this saves everyone, vendor included, much time and money. Respectable wholesalers are happy to provide such information; shysters are not.

Second caveat: be sure that the prospective wholesaler actually does have some book inventory on hand; certain wholesalers practice a quaint practice called drop shipping. The wholesaler who drop ships takes a library's order and transmits it to the appropriate publisher or publishers. The publisher in turn fills the orders and ships the books to the library—but bills the wholesaler, who then bills the library. Note that drop shippers do not warehouse any books.

This is an absurd process at best. Why pay someone to do practically nothing, or at least nothing more than add to the time it takes to receive the books? Any wholesaler who drop ships should be avoided like the plague. (It should be noted that *Literary Market Place* is a useful tool for determining who the few book drop shippers are; it lists most wholesalers, their specialties, the number of books and titles they stock, and whether they drop ship.)

PROMPT ORDER FULFILLMENT

When dealing with a reputable wholesaler who maintains an adequate inventory, librarians can reasonably expect receipt of an initial shipment of 75 to 80 percent of the materials ordered within two weeks. Anything lower than this fulfillment percentage is, as a rule, unacceptable and should not be tolerated. On certain occasions, however, a library may send a special order for books that are not likely to be stocked regularly by the wholesaler, perhaps to create a special collection or to give greater depth to an area of the collection; in a case like this, it may be understandable for the vendor to take longer to fill the order, but this should be the exception, not the rule.

A few really good wholesalers guarantee shipment of most or all of a library's order within forty-eight hours of receipt, and more often than not achieve that goal; for the rest, two weeks is more realistic. Then the vendor has time to obtain the unfulfilled balance of the order—the books not in stock or the more esoteric titles—within the library's stipulated ship or cancel period, usually ninety days. Consistently failing to meet this standard, however, should mean that the vendor be dropped, because such performance is inexcusable and serves only to alienate frustrated library patrons who can't understand why a book ordered two or three months ago is still not on the shelf.

ACCURATE ORDER FULFILLMENT

Just as librarians have a right to expect promptness in order fulfillment, they have the right to expect accuracy. There is no reason why a wholesaler should constantly err on titles or editions shipped, particularly when ISBNs are given, or in number of copies shipped. Returns, claims, and debit/credit procedures are a very costly part of the acquisitions process for both libraries and vendors, because they require a lot of staff time. Any vendor whose fulfillment error rate exceeds 1 or 2 percent should not be in business; any library book purchaser who accepts such shoddy performance should be doing something else. Certainly errors will and do occur, but again, they should be the rare exception to the rule. Careful monitoring of vendor performance is the only way for the acquisitions librarian to determine which vendors take the library's business seriously enough to fill orders accurately as well as promptly.

ACCURATE ORDER-STATUS REPORTING

A few years ago at an ALA Annual Conference, a very large wholesaler was exhibiting its wares and touting its long tradition of excellent service to libraries. At a meeting nearby on vendor/library relations, an author of several children's books was speaking; she complained that one of her books was being reported as out of print by that same wholesaler. Not only was the book still in print, however, but copies of it were also being displayed at her publisher's booth only a few dozen feet away from the wholesaler's display.

To say that the audience was incensed is an understatement, and rightfully so. This incident confirmed what a lot of astute librarians have long suspected: that status reports from some wholesalers do not reflect reality but what wholesalers would *like* librarians to believe is the reality. Accurate status reporting is essential so that the acquisitions librarian can decide whether to reorder the book from another wholesaler or directly from the publisher. Since reordering is both costly and time consuming, the decision is not made lightly. And it is extremely frustrating to be unable to obtain needed items for the library's collection, but when this happens not because such items are truly unavailable but because a vendor is either careless enough or venal enough to mislead its customers, then it is intolerable.

Two decades ago I wrote an article on the pros and cons of dealing with wholesalers. In preparation for writing it, I asked the staff to carefully monitor the wholesalers' status reports submitted to our system. It turned out to be a time-consuming but very revealing process. The results were as follows:

- For books reported as *out of print* (OP), wholesalers' reports were accurate approximately 60 percent of the time.
- For books reported as *out of stock* (OS) with the publisher, wholesalers' reports were accurate less than 20 percent of the time.

In other words, fewer than half of the status reports received from some of the major wholesalers with whom we were then doing business were accurate; one of these vendors was at that time the largest book wholesaler in the United States.

Why do these vendors report so poorly on book status? They say it is because the information they receive from publishers is inaccurate. But my study based its validity on calling publishers directly to confirm the status data reported to us by wholesalers, and publishers indicated that the wholesalers' reports were rarely valid. It follows, then, that either certain wholesalers are incredibly careless in their reporting, or that some wholesalers deliberately misreport in order to increase profit by selling only what is in their warehouses (I use the present tense here because the problem still exists, although some—not all—of the worst offenders have gone out of business).

It takes both time and money to fill nonstock orders. When a library orders a book that the vendor does not have on hand, the vendor must go through all the same steps of ordering, processing, shipping, and billing that the acquisitions librarian goes through in acquiring a book. It takes a lot less time (and money) to simply report that the book is OP or OSI, or simply that the vendor cannot supply the title and cancel the library's order—with the near certainty that most librarians will accept this report in good faith and spend the money on something that the wholesaler *does* have in stock. The wise library purchaser will monitor wholesaler status reports as carefully and consistently as all other aspects of vendor performance. There is no excuse for continuing poor performance in this area, and vendors who persist in this less-than-savory process should be dropped.

REASONABLE AND COMPETITIVE DISCOUNTS

This is and should be one of the areas of greatest concern to astute librarians, because the discount is something that can very easily be manipulated and abused, especially for the more naïve members of the library profession. We have already seen that publishers' discount policies in dealing with libraries can be capricious and arbitrary, ranging from the eminently fair and reasonable to the downright discriminatory and totally absurd. The same is true for wholesalers, except that their actions are not always so obvious.

The wisdom of Daniel Melcher's statement at the beginning of this chapter becomes clear when one carefully examines the various discount structures employed by wholesalers and begins to ask the right questions. The answers to those questions can affect a library's purchasing power in a very positive way by ensuring that the library is not paying more than necessary for its books:

- What is a reasonable discount?
- What is discriminatory discounting?
- What kind of discounts am I receiving, and how do they compare with those given to other libraries with similar book budgets and buying patterns?

In *Melcher on Acquisition*, Daniel Melcher states that effective book buying depends on a good working knowledge of the economics of wholesaling—not what wholesalers would like you to believe about

Table 8.1 Discounts to Wholesalers	
Number of Copies*	**Discount from Publisher**
1 copy	10–20%
2–4 copies	25–33$\frac{1}{3}$%
5–24 copies	40%
25–99 copies	41%
100–249 copies	42%
250–499 copies	43%
500–999 copies	44%
1,000+ copies**	46%

*Do not have to be all one title; can be assorted.
**On occasion, the discount for more than 1,000 copies can rise as high as 56 percent, but 46 percent is the norm.
Source: ABA Bookbuyers Handbook (1997).

wholesaling economics, but what the facts are. And those facts are simple: book wholesaling is a business with a rather low profit margin or return on investment (estimated at an average of 3 to 5 percent; food supermarket profits are about the only others that are lower, at only about 1 percent). Because the profit margin is low, wholesalers must, like other businesses, sell a *lot* of books that were sold to them on a high discount basis, enough to ensure maximum profit from sheer volume, or sell fewer lower-discount books. Those who ignore these simple facts do so at their peril; the demise during the 1970s and early 1980s of a dozen major book wholesaling companies—Campbell & Hall, Ancorp, Richard Abel, Charles Clark, Imperial Books, Huntting, and Dimondstein, among others—revealed to librarians just how difficult the business is. And although the market today is dominated by Ingram Books, Baker & Taylor, Blackwell, and a few midsized, specialized, and smaller firms, even they have had rough times over the last few decades. (A selective list of currently operating wholesalers appears in Appendix A at the end of this book.)

Why is the profit margin in book wholesaling so slim? The answer lies in the rigid discount schedule that publishers give their wholesaler customers, which defines (in most cases) what the wholesaler can charge its library customers. A look at a typical trade-book discount schedule (see Table 8.1) gives some idea of what wholesalers pay for books.

Since the bulk of a wholesaler's book orders for trade-book purchases fall into the 40 to 46 percent discount range, the smart wholesaler will try to accumulate orders for any given publisher to attain the maximum discount possible.

But the real problem for the wholesaler is this: if a wholesaler wants library business, the company must compete with the discounts that the books' producers—publishers—give to libraries that buy direct from them. In most cases, these publisher discounts are lower, usually 10 to 25 percent for their library customers, but some will be 40 percent or higher—mainly for larger libraries with high-volume purchases. If every book the wholesaler buys is discounted by the publisher at 46 percent, this leaves the wholesaler only a 6 percent margin. Out of that 6 percent come all the customary business expenses that must be met before a profit is earned, such as buildings, salaries, heat, lights, telephone, and freight. Clearly, wholesalers must do everything possible to minimize cost and maximize profit in order to stay in business.

There are a number of ways to do this, some of which are proper and others which smack of impropriety. Cutting costs is the most obvious, and this certainly has been successful for some vendors. But cost cutting often is at the expense of service to library customers, as in the previous example of reporting books not in the warehouse as OP or OSI.

Reducing warehouse inventory is another way to reduce costs, but again service suffers when the library does not receive books on a timely basis because the wholesaler has to order them from the publisher. Decreasing their discounts to libraries may also reduce wholesalers' costs, but it also may alienate library customers and ultimately result in the loss of valuable business. Imposing exorbitant "shipping and handling" charges may bring in some wonderful pure profit: one wholesaler sold the library where I worked six videocassettes at $75.00 each, and charged the library $45.00 *each* for postage and handling— a total of $270.00 over and above the $450.00 cost of the materials (that was *some* handling).

It should be noted that wholesalers are not alone in using this ploy. In 1987, the R. R. Bowker Company announced that henceforth a flat 5 percent of the invoice total would be charged for "shipping and handling"; this meant that on a $10,000 order for Bowker reference books, a library would pay $500 in shipping costs—even though the actual cost of shipping the books by common carrier was only about $140. Even worse, however, was the fact that the customer who chose to buy those reference materials in CD-ROM format would pay *the same amount* for shipping and handling—even though the actual cost of shipping a few compact discs by first-class mail or UPS amounted to less than $20—leaving Bowker with a pure profit on just this one invoice of $480. Needless to say, library customers were irate, and after some months of pressure, Bowker rescinded this absurd policy.

While all these cost-cutting, profit-increasing tactics are somewhat questionable, at least they are fairly straightforward. But wholesalers have found a number of other ways to increase profits by playing not-so-straightforward games with discounts. The most common of these are

1. inflating book prices or reporting phony discounts from publishers
2. overcharging for certain bindings
3. offering outlandishly high discounts to libraries that require bids for their business
4. establishing "across-the-board" discount structures.

Each can be illustrated very simply and each is an actual incident that occurred.

Inflating Prices

Not long ago a library ordered several copies of a paperback title from a major wholesaler. The books were back ordered and eventually arrived with the invoice. The library had planned to pay $6.95 for each of the books. The wholesaler charged $8.95 each, however—even though the printed cover price was still $6.95. The discount given on the wholesaler's invoice was 10 percent, and the code indicated the reason for this was that this was a short discount title from the publisher. However, someone at the wholesaler's warehouse had inadvertently left the invoice that was sent to the wholesaler in one of the books. It showed that the net price of the books was $6.95 each, and the publisher's discount to the wholesaler was a whopping 52 percent—not exactly a "short" discount. Another wholesaler of art books offered the library a flat 10 percent discount on his titles, since he got "only 20 percent" from the books' publishers. The library's business relationship with him came to a rather abrupt halt when an astute staff member discovered a copy of one of his publisher invoices at the bottom of a carton; the document indicated that he was receiving a 56 percent discount on each and every book ordered. Understandably, his company went out of business once the word got around to a few of his bigger customers. And in case anyone doubts that this kind of thing still goes on, *Publishers Weekly* reported in its February 10, 1997 (p. 17) issue that a small publisher had "been trying for more than two years to learn why books he sold to B&T at a trade discount were being sold to stores and libraries at only a 5% short discount." Apparently he never did find out.

Binding Overcharges

Overcharging for certain bindings is a scam practiced frequently by wholesalers who sell children's books. Hardcover children's books usually have one of three kinds of binding: a nearly indestructible sewn *library binding*, which is usually discounted to wholesalers at 25 percent because of the added cost to produce this type of binding; a *reinforced binding*, which is not as sturdy as library binding but stronger than the third kind of binding; and the same *trade binding* used for most adult trade hardcover books. Both reinforced and trade bindings are sold to wholesalers at the standard trade discount of up to 46 percent, depending on volume. The rub comes when some wholesalers arbitrarily decide to classify reinforced bindings (sometimes called single bindings) as library bindings, and thus are in a position to extend short discounts to their library customers. As a result, the library's discount on reinforced bindings usually ends up between 6 and 13 percent, the same discount received on a true library binding, which of course means that the wholesaler's profit has jumped from a range of 12 to 19 percent to one more than three times that much. The smart librarian will not buy reinforced bindings from wholesalers who pull this stunt, but will go to another wholesaler who doesn't or go direct to the publisher and get the publisher's full trade discount—which, even if it is only 20 percent for libraries, is better than what the wholesaler is offering.

Discounts on Bids

Some unfortunate librarians are required by law to obtain bids for their business. Still others get bids because they think they will receive better discounts as a result; these latter librarians are not so much unfortunate as hopelessly naïve, for this is where the less-than-honest wholesaler can indulge in hanky-panky of the first order. Keeping in mind the usual maximum trade discount the wholesaler receives, what should the librarian think of the wholesaler's representative who offers a 44, 45, or 46 percent discount on trade books in exchange for all the library's business? What we should think is that this person either is a fool, a knave, or a liar. And the librarian who believes this kind of pie-in-the-sky promise is just as foolish as the sales pitch. In the first place, since most librarians buy a lot of trade books, are we to believe that a wholesaler is going to give up all or nearly all of the profit from trade-book sales? And since librarians also buy a lot of nontrade books, many of which carry smaller publisher discounts than trade books, what is the wholesaler going to do about those prices and discounts? What will prevent the wholesaler from simply supplying those books on which a greater profit is to be made, reporting the less profitable titles as OP or OSI, and letting orders for those titles sit in a file until the library's cancellation date is reached?

Simply put, getting bids is unwise, to say the least, whether or not one has to do it. If you must ask for bids, however, get an agreement *in writing* that spells out *all* discount terms, minimally acceptable levels of order fulfillment, and specific types of books that the wholesaler cannot or will not supply. Then monitor that contract with extreme care; if you don't, you'll end up paying more than you should for too many books, seeing holes develop in the collection where books ordered are not being provided, or both.

Across-the-Board Discounts

At one time or another, just about every wholesaler tries to convince its customers that they'll be a lot better off if they accept a "generous" blanket discount on all materials purchased than if they get one discount for trade books, another on paperbacks, still another for short-discount titles, and so on. What usually happens with this "generic" discount, however, is that the wholesaler makes out big—with the library paying to make it possible. To illustrate, I once received a letter from a large wholesaler (and usually a good one) stating that henceforth all books sold by them to libraries would be discounted at a flat 15 percent rate. What did this mean to us? Simply that buying books from that vendor had just become prohibitive. Here's why: As a major public library system, the library for which I was working spent more than half of its $6 million book budget on trade and paperback books, all of which were discounted at an average of approximately 36 to 37 percent (since much of this business was done directly with publishers, some of whom offered full trade discounts but many more of whom offered smaller discounts to their library customers). Only about 20 percent of the budget was spent on limited discount books, those discounted from 15 percent down to no discount at all. In other words, with the wholesaler's new flat 15 percent discount, the library would be losing up to 22 percent of the discount it had been receiving on 50 percent of the books purchased, and in return would gain 5 to 15 percent on 20 percent of the total books purchased. Even P. T. Barnum would be hard-pressed to find a sucker foolish enough to swallow that one.

STRICT ADHERENCE TO LIBRARY POLICIES

Libraries, like most other institutions, operate in certain ways and within certain parameters that are defined by policy that may be as formal as a written statement or as informal as a set of procedures that everyone understands and accepts. Whether the policy is formal or informal, however, the vendor who does business with the library is expected to follow these "rules of the game" at all times. It behooves the acquisitions librarian to put these policies in writing and to make them available to anyone who wishes to do business with the library, *and* to monitor how well each vendor does in meeting the library's requirements.

Vendors, both publishers and wholesalers, frequently complain about the diversity among libraries' requirements. Library A wants a six-part invoice arranged by ISBN, Library B a three-part bill with titles listed in alphabetical order; Library C wants unfilled orders canceled in ninety days, but Library D will settle for 120 days; Library E requires that vendors ship all materials by UPS, while Library F specifies that the vendor must use the USPS's library rate; and so it goes.

It may be true that there is little uniformity as far as library policies go, but there are often good reasons why such diversity exists. Different governing bodies and agencies at various levels impose certain requirements on libraries, for example, and laws governing purchases vary from locality to locality. A wise vendor accepts this diversity and follows whatever reasonable strictures the library mandates. (Further discussion of the library's obligations to vendors appears in Chapter 9.)

OTHER SERVICES

Some of the greatest advantages in dealing with wholesalers are the extra services many offer to their library customers. For small and large libraries alike, such items as catalog cards and nominally priced processing kits or fully processed books can free staff for other duties and thus become a serious budget consideration. Larger libraries also often use services such as gathering plans: lease plans, standing-order plans, approval plans, and blanket-order plans. Except for lease plans, which are used primarily by public libraries, the other gathering plans are most useful in university or research libraries and in some special libraries. (Further discussion of the pros and cons of gathering plans follows in Chapter 10.)

A RAY OF LIGHT

While there are a lot of good reasons for library book purchasers to buy many or even most of their books from wholesalers, these vendors must be carefully chosen, constantly monitored, and dropped when and if it becomes necessary. For some reason, librarians seem loath to discuss the companies that provide them with books, but open discussion of their strengths and weaknesses is the only way to get rid of the rascals and keep the good folks in business.

Earlier in this chapter I mentioned an article I wrote on the pros and cons of dealing with wholesalers. The article was preceded by a survey of 320 libraries of all types and sizes on major aspects of their dealings with wholesalers: discounts, order fulfillment, accuracy, and others. The results of the survey indicated an almost unbelievable discrepancy among libraries as to discounts given. For example, one library with a book budget of nearly $1 million received a 38 percent discount on trade hardcovers from one of the largest wholesalers, while a nearby library with a budget of $12,000 received a 41 percent discount. A very small library in the South was given a 13 percent discount on library editions, while a major school system in the Cleveland, Ohio, area got only a 7.5 percent discount on those same books. With few exceptions, none of the 320 respondents were satisfied with their discounts or felt that they were fair or reasonable, and both those feelings and this sort of imbalance remains today. Nonetheless, most who responded indicated that they would continue to buy from wholesalers and felt there was a real need for this service.

The fact remains, however, that we are doing neither good wholesalers nor our library colleagues a favor by continuing to give library dollars to those companies not deserving of our support. They are the wholesalers who will do anything to get our business; who swear they can supply any book in print the day after tomorrow at less cost than any of the competition. They are the wholesalers whose representatives seem to believe that they deserve our business if they take us to expensive lunches or dinners often enough. They are also the wholesalers who overcharge us, misrepresent their inventories, and fill only those orders that make them the greatest profit. In short, they are the snake-oil salespeople of the book industry and should be avoided like the plague by those who purchase books for libraries, especially when it involves using taxpayers' money to pay for them, as it usually does.

Good wholesalers do not play games with their library customers based on inflated discount promises; they do not give Library A one discount and Library B another when both libraries' purchasing patterns and volumes are similar. They may never take you to lunch, but let their good service be their sales pitch. (And is there a librarian out there who really believes that all those "free" lunches aren't paid for by the rest of us?)

Good wholesalers clearly state their discount structure in their ads for all to see. They give librarians access to their inventory through regular (usually weekly) warehouse-inventory status reports on microfiche, disc, or online. They fill each and every order that is possible to fill. In short, they conduct business with their customers professionally—which is the only way we should accept. The ray of light is that there are a lot of those professionals out there; we just have to find them and support their efforts as best we can.

9 LIBRARY/VENDOR RELATIONS

In an ideal world, there would be no need for this chapter. Judging from both experience and the stories one hears, though, the real world of library book purchasing is far from ideal. Therefore, a discussion of some of the things that library book purchasers can do to make the buyer/seller relationship a more mutually productive one is in order.

PROVIDE ADEQUATE BIBLIOGRAPHIC DATA

Asking a book vendor to supply a title without adequate data is about as sensible as writing to L. L. Bean and asking that company to send you a sweater. The following basic bibliographic data that a vendor needs in order to process your order accurately and efficiently should be programmed into the purchase order for every title ordered:

1. *Title.* This should be exact enough for the vendor to identify the precise item being ordered; frequently, subtitles will further clarify what you want. In the case of common titles, such as *Ivanhoe* or *Little Red Riding Hood*, more information must, of course, be given, such as edition or illustrator.
2. *The author's, authors', or editor's name*, with surname first.
3. *Publisher.* Enough of the publisher's name should be given to clarify exactly which publisher's product is being ordered. For example, it is not necessary to spell out "Harcourt, Brace"; Harcourt is enough. But be careful of abbreviations; does "Har" mean "Harcourt," "HarperCollins," "Hart Publishing," or some other house?
4. *Format.* Specify format exactly. Do you want hardcover or paperback, especially if both formats are available? Do you want a children's book with library binding, or will a trade edition do?
5. *Edition.* If currency is important, specify the edition wanted, for example, "6th ed.," "revised ed.," "latest ed." Note special requirements such as "text ed.," "large print ed.," "teacher's ed."
6. *Price.* Give the most recent list price, that is, the price assigned by the publisher.

7. *ISBN* (International Standard Book Number). This is probably the most important element in bibliographic identification. Each ISBN is unique and identifies a specific book as to title, author, edition, publisher, binding—everything. Even if other elements of bibliographic data given on your purchase order are inaccurate, when the ISBN is correct, your chances of getting the book you want are very good. The ISBN has some drawbacks, however; probably the most serious that it is a ten-digit number, which is easy to record inaccurately; in addition, publishers often use the ISBN in an arbitrary and often capricious way (as a method of inventory control, for example). With the increasing use of electronic and online book ordering, however, the ISBN is *the* major bibliographic identifier. (An excellent brief overview of the ISBN can be found in the prefatory matter in Volume 1 of any print edition of *Books in Print* or any recent edition of *The Bowker Annual*.)

In addition to these bibliographic data, the vendor needs to know exactly how many copies are being ordered. It is helpful to note whether a set or only specific elements of a set are being ordered: are you ordering the entire set of *Grove's Dictionary of Music and Musicians*? If so, specify, as "1 set" or "6 vols." If only a particular volume of a set is required, specify that: "Vol. 5 only."

The vendor also needs an accurate purchase order number. To enable both vendor and library to keep track of which particular order for a title is being shipped or is being paid for, a unique purchase order number is necessary for each transaction. Finally, any other pertinent information or specific instructions for the vendor should be clearly noted. Specify clearly on the purchase order whether the materials are to be shipped via UPS or common carrier only, or by USPS library rate. If books are to be billed to one address and shipped to another, note this as well. Finally, reiterating the library's cancellation requirements on every purchase order is a wise move—"Cancel orders not filled within 90 days of purchase order date," for example.

PLACE TIMELY ORDERS

As has been noted in earlier chapters, it is vital to order materials with the greatest alacrity possible given current trends in publishing. Print runs of books get smaller all the time, which means that books go out of stock more rapidly, and books are being declared out of print sooner than ever before. Therefore, waiting for weeks or months to place an order is the surest way to guarantee that many of the books you want will not be available. Orders should be placed on a weekly basis, even daily if at all possible. A monthly order cycle is bad enough, but those institutions such as school, academic, and certain public libraries—which order books only once or twice a year—should be forewarned that fill rates for such orders will be unbelievably low—through no fault of the vendor, in most cases.

SET REASONABLE REQUIREMENTS FOR FORMS

Both publishers and wholesalers complain that there is no consistency among libraries regarding the number of invoice copies required. Some are satisfied with the original and one or two copies; others require as many as an original and six or seven copies. The latter requirement is foolish. First, it may cost the vendor half again as much for an eight-part invoice form as for a three- or four-part form; does anyone really believe that that cost won't be passed on to all the company's customers in some way or another? Second, why does *any* library need or want seven copies of an invoice? Do you really plan to *do something* with each of them—file them and then, later, unfile them? Since office cost studies indicate that the real cost of filing a single item now exceeds $14.00 per item, couldn't staff time be better used for something more productive than shuffling thousands of pieces of paper around? Any library that requires more than three copies of any form the vendor provides has real problems with operational cost-effectiveness and needs to examine its clerical operation very carefully—for its own benefit as well as that of its vendors.

BE (REASONABLY) FLEXIBLE ABOUT PRICES

A few years ago a wholesaler told me of a library that returned a number of copies of a major best-selling title because it came in at a per copy price of $2 more than the librarian had expected. In this case, as it happened, the vendor was not at fault because the publisher had decided to increase the book's cover price by $2.00 to "celebrate" the millionth copy sold in hardcover, unbelievable as that sounds. (Food for thought, though! See Chapter 5 on costing book prices out and economies of scale in the book industry. What a rip-off.) This demonstrates how difficult it is for libraries to accurately figure out what the cost of a book being ordered will be.

Most librarians use *Books in Print* (*BIP*) as their source for prices, but on the day the print version arrives in the library thousands of its prices are out of date. (The CD-ROM version was an improvement, but librarians reported on the Internet that they had problems using it; the only real solution is to use the online version available through Infotrac, or Bowker's new Booksinprint.com 2000, but these may be financially out of reach for smaller libraries.) When publishers change (usually raise) prices during that lengthy period between collecting and publishing, *BIP* cannot reflect these changes until its new edition or supplement. This problem is particularly acute for purchasers of scientific and technical books; those prices increase more rapidly and more erratically than almost any others. Those libraries that can afford to are much better off using *BIP* online, as noted above, since updating a database is much simpler and faster than updating a set of books or even a CD-ROM. Then there are the various wholesalers' online databases, which are updated at least weekly and sometimes even more often than that. A further alternative is to use the Internet to access one of the big commercial retailers' databases, such as Amazon.com's or Barnes&noble.com's; their prices are updated almost daily.

In short, then, the library book purchaser cannot be completely rigid about prices and must be prepared to recognize that predicting the price of a book is, at best, an educated guess. To return materials to the vendor because of price changes—without checking to see whether the changes are legitimate—may cost both the vendor and the library a lot of money. An easy way to resolve some of these problems is to stipulate in your agreements with vendors that a price increase of up to a certain amount (say $5.00 or $10.00), or a certain percentage (2 percent or 5 percent) is acceptable, but if increases are greater than that, the order should be canceled. (It is still wise to spot-check increases, especially if you notice that everything you're ordering is going up by exactly the limit you set!)

ALLOW ADEQUATE CANCELLATION PERIOD

If you want to obtain a reasonable fulfillment rate on titles ordered, your library must give the vendor enough time to complete the order. For most books, a period of ninety days from purchase order date should be the maximum allowed. This gives the wholesaler time to fill a good percentage of the order from the warehouse inventory within a few days or a few weeks at most. It also allows the wholesaler time to try to obtain those titles that are not stocked in the warehouse and to report on titles that are simply not available despite the wholesaler's best efforts to obtain them.

The ninety-day period is not enough time for the vendor to obtain some categories of books, however. Most books published in Britain and Western European countries may require up to 180 days, while books from Eastern Europe, Asia, and the rest of the world (except Canada) may take even longer—up to a year, in some cases. Then, too, there are a few reprint publishers (who reprint out-of-print titles) who do not go for a new printing of a title until they have accumulated a minimum number of orders. Allowing a period of a year before cancellation of certain reprints, therefore, is not unreasonable.

Finally, the librarian may have occasion to use an out-of-print-books vendor who will attempt to procure OP titles from whatever sources may be able to supply them. This process may be a very long one (and a very costly one, as a rule), so allowing the vendor sufficient time to do a proper search is essential.

MAKE PROMPT PAYMENT

A vendor has a right to expect prompt payment for goods delivered. In the case of libraries, prompt payment usually means within thirty to sixty days of delivery. In some cases, vendors offer substantial savings to libraries that pay their bills fast. This may take the form of an extra discount if an invoice is paid within a stipulated period or before the end of the month (EOM). How beneficial this can be is illustrated by an example from my local library system, whose major wholesaler offers an extra 2 percent discount for all invoices paid by EOM. Since the system spends close to $1 million each year with this vendor, paying bills promptly realizes for them a savings of some $20,000 annually.

If a library does *not* pay most of its bills within sixty days of receiving materials (provided, of course, that both the shipment and the invoice are accurate), then something is wrong with the library's accounting methods. This internal failure should not be visited upon the vendor as a punishment for the library's failings. If the responsibility for the library's late payment lies with the vendor, however—particularly if the vendor consistently ships inaccurate materials or makes too many errors on invoices—the vendor should be reconsidered and perhaps dropped in favor of another who can provide more satisfactory and accurate service.

HAVE A REASONABLE RETURNS POLICY

Librarians do not usually return books to vendors unless there is good reason: the book is defective, it is the wrong title, or the library's cancellation period has been exceeded by the time the book arrives and the money to pay for it has been unencumbered. Some librarians do abuse returns, however; a light stain on a page (if it does not impair the book's readability) or a slightly dented corner of the cover does not necessarily mean that a book is defective. By the same token, a best-seller that circulates thirty-eight times and then begins to fall apart is not necessarily defective either. And a book that has a missing signature or misnumbered pages that are not discovered until years after the book was purchased should not be returned; instead an examination of the library's selection policy might be in order.

When returns are necessary, the librarian should clearly state what the problem is and whether the library is taking a credit on the invoice or is willing to wait for the vendor to supply a replacement copy. Some vendors make the returns process easier by providing their customers with "instant credit" via self-credit forms that can be filled out and sent to the publisher/wholesaler without the delay and fuss caused by adjusting the invoice. This is a great time saver and a money saver as well, for both the library and the vendor.

However, it may be most cost efficient to simply write off certain materials instead of returning them, thus again saving money for both library and vendor. For example, a branch once asked my system's ordering department to return a fifteen-cent pamphlet for credit because the ink was smeared, but quickly backed off when we said we would then have to bill the branch for the $21.00 in clerical time it would cost us to do this (to say nothing of how much it would cost the vendor). In the end, if the librarian has ordered a book in error, and has accepted it and processed it, it is the librarian's obligation *not* to return the book. If the book has not been processed, however, the librarian should request permission to return it; such permission usually is readily granted by responsible vendors.

MAINTAIN PROFESSIONAL STANDARDS

In Ohio, a library director (now deceased) became famous among sales representatives around the state for free-loading expensive lunches and dinners by dangling the bait that he *might* consider doing business with them but would first like to discuss this—"over dinner, perhaps." This kind of practice is highly unprofessional, certainly unethical, and probably illegal in libraries and universities in many states, to say the least; plus, it does nothing to enhance the image of the library profession.

Just how does the library book purchaser handle meal (and other) invitations—which frequently are extended? First, keep them to a minimum. Second, remember that this is an accepted way of doing business, as long as business is discussed during the course of a meal (an Internal Revenue Service expense-account requirement, incidentally, for any business person who wishes to claim such expenses as client meals). At the same time, keep in mind that accepting such invitations imposes no obligations. As I said in Chapter 8, any sales representative who actually believes that a free lunch or dinner will buy a library's business is a fool.

Then there is the problem of handling the salesperson who calls to make an appointment to discuss the possibility of doing business with the library. Since acquisitions librarians are usually busy people, the decision must be made as to whether or not to use precious time in such discussion. If you are fairly sure that you won't be getting anything new or better than you are getting from your current vendors, it is best to say that you have no reason to make any changes at this point but will keep the potential vendor in mind in case the situation changes. The alternative response, of course, is to make the appointment, listen to the pitch, and decide whether to give the company a try for a specified length of time. Either way, the important thing is to be honest with the sales representative; there is nothing to be gained from wasting either your time or the salesperson's.

Another situation that should be dealt with directly is when a representative "drops in" to call on the librarian, without the courtesy of calling in advance for an appointment. This is not only annoying but also insulting, implying as it does that the librarian can just drop everything to see the rep and have a cozy schmooze. When this happens, it is best to say that you see no one without an appointment; the lesson is soon learned. One has to wonder what would happen if that salesperson tried to just "drop in" on the family's doctor or dentist a few times.

Finally, there is the matter of fairness in placing orders. A librarian once told me that he sent all his "problem" orders to one particular vendor: low-discount titles; association publications, which are often difficult to locate; foreign titles; and titles that had been reported as OP or OSI by his primary wholesaler. This kind of practice was and is very unfair and usually results in a very low fill rate from the hapless vendor. In this case, the vendor's profits were small, and it wasn't long before he went out of business. Making such unreasonable demands on certain vendors is not only a poor way to do business but also very unprofessional and should be avoided at all cost.

What this chapter is really saying is very simple: in all relations with vendors, the acquisitions librarian must be as fair, impartial, scrupulous, professional, and courteous as in any other business dealings. More than a decade and a half ago, the American Library Association published a monograph, *Guidelines for Handling Library Orders for In-Print Monographic Publications*, which spelled it all out very nicely: "Libraries and bookdealers conduct their business on a contractual basis, whether formal or informal. The object is to provide the best possible service to the library at reasonable cost. . . . All successful relationships depend on the goodwill and cooperation of both parties." Amen to that!

10 THE ORDERING PROCESS

Probably the best definition of library acquisitions is the one that G. Edward Evans used in his *Developing Library Collections* way back in 1979. He said that "Acquisitions work [is] the process by which the library physically secures . . . the items that selection personnel have identified as desirable additions to the collection." That ordering process that Evans defined so succinctly is basically a very simple process. With the single exception of an added layer (the fund-accounting procedure), book ordering by libraries is, or at least should be, no more complicated than it is in bookstores. What has happened, though, is that too many libraries have added too many layers of meaningless procedure to this simple process, with the result that they are spending more on getting books than on the books themselves. This is particularly ironic and patently foolish when we continually bemoan the fact that we can only spend 10 or 12 percent of our funds on materials, and the rest goes to personnel costs and other costs of running our institutions. Perhaps it is time to take a good look at our procedural sacred cows. As Melcher says in his *Melcher on Acquisition*:

> It is completely absurd that we couldn't study the hundreds of procedures now in use and boil them down to a handful at most. Perhaps we couldn't legislate the sillier variations out of existence, but we could go farther than we have to shame them out of existence. . . . We could use a little less of "But feel free to do it your own way . . . ." And a little more of "Look, stop being a damn fool." (p. 27)

FUNCTIONS AND GOALS

In simplest terms, the function of the acquisitions department is to obtain the books and other library materials that those responsible for selection of such materials have deemed worthy of inclusion in the library's collection. While some of these materials may be acquired through such means as gifts or exchanging books with other libraries, the vast majority are acquired through purchase.

The goal of the acquisitions department defines its purchase function. This goal should be to perform whatever activities are necessary to insure that:

- materials are obtained as quickly as possible
- materials are obtained as inexpensively as possible

- materials are obtained with a high degree of accuracy
- work processes and procedures are as simple as possible to keep the unit cost of securing materials as low as possible
- monitoring and control of expenditures are maintained
- necessary fund accounting is maintained and accurately reported
- payments to vendors for materials received are made in a timely manner
- vendor performance is monitored and evaluated on an ongoing basis
- cordial and professional relations with vendors are maintained
- accurate and timely reporting on availability/nonavailability of materials is transmitted to those responsible for selection and collection development

The acquisitions department that understands its function within the larger organization of the library and attains its goals on a consistent basis is very likely to meet every library's ultimate goal: to provide the proper materials to supply the information needs of its patron community. This goal applies to every library, regardless of type. The academic library provides for the information needs of students, faculty, and scholars. The special library provides for the needs of those within a given profession or field of endeavor. The school library provides for student and teacher needs. The public library strives to supply the information needs of the general population in the community it serves. It is vitally important for all members of the acquisitions staff to keep in mind that, even though they may not serve the public directly, their goal is the same as their library's goal. Nothing less will do.

STEPS IN THE ORDER PROCESS

Selection and acquisitions are terms that are often used interchangeably in everyday library parlance. The two processes are closely related but, in fact, they are not interchangeable. And it is rare for the selection and acquisitions functions to be performed by the same staff in most libraries, especially larger ones. Selectors, for the most part, are those who choose the materials for the collection. Acquisitions staff are those who obtain the materials chosen by the selectors; together, they are responsible for developing the library's collection.

Once the selectors have made their choices and recorded them, the work of the acquisitions department—the ordering process—begins. There are eight basic steps to this process. Exact details may vary from institution to institution and whether the library has automated its acquisitions process, but the basic procedures are common to all library materials purchasing and so require some discussion.

STEP 1: FILING/COLLATING/TALLYING ORDERS

In some libraries each book requested is noted on a request form that is transmitted to the acquisitions department, filed according to the department's procedures (as in alphabetically by title or author), and then searched as to availability and possible duplication within the collection. In other libraries, selectors choose from lists of titles prepared and sent to the acquisitions department by specialists in or out of house; these lists may be hard copy (paper) or, if the library has an automated system, sent online. Other lists may contain titles of books that were obtained from various kinds of gathering plans such as standing-order plans, approval plans, or Greenaway plans, and still others may be compilations of patron requests.

Whatever form the request for materials takes, in order to perform the next step—verification—certain pieces of information are required by the acquisitions department: title, author, publisher, ISBN, edition, price, year of publication, number of copies, and name of the selector or agency requesting the book. In libraries where more than one fund may be charged for the books, the librarian must specify which fund is to be encumbered (for example, adult, juvenile, young adult, special funds of one sort or another). It is usually noted whether the book ordered is for reference or for circulation.

STEP 2: SEARCHING/VERIFICATION

Once the request forms or lists have been received and filed or entered online according to the library's general methods, the next step is to establish the availability or nonavailability of the item requested by searching whatever databases to which the library has access. These databases may be in print form, as in *Books in Print*; on microfiche; on CD-ROM, as in *Books in Print on Disc*; or may be an online database such as Booksinprint.com or the OCLC database. They may be wholesalers' databases, such as Baker & Taylor's Libris 2020. Further sources are commercial online databases accessible through the Internet such as Amazon.com or Barnes&noble.com. Whatever is used, the acquisitions staff is simply trying to find out if there is a chance of getting the book: Is it reasonably certain that this particular work is available? If the bibliographic data given on the request form or list are accurate and adequate, determining availability should be a simple enough task.

Recent developments in software have made the search-and-order function even simpler. It is possible to search a title and at the same time assign the vendor and transmit the order electronically. OCLC's pilot acquisitions program was one of the first of these, but it proved too costly and too cumbersome for many libraries and so was subsequently discontinued except for certain academic libraries. Today, however, a number of wholesalers have extensive software packages that enable the user to search not only current titles but also forthcoming titles; Ingram Book Company, Baker & Taylor, and many others offer this service, as well as online ordering capability (see Appendix A, List of Selected Wholesalers). Using them, it is simplicity itself to verify availability and order a title almost simultaneously. The problem is that not all vendors are equipped to receive electronic orders, but the success of those who are is rapidly leading others—even publishers, who are rarely on the cutting edge of technology—to jump on the bandwagon.

A word of clarification: in books on the acquisitions process, the terms "searching" and "verification" are often used almost interchangeably. In his *Developing Library Collections* (Libraries Unlimited, 1979, p.199), however, G. Edward Evans states: "Bibliographic searching/verification consists of two elements. One element is the establishment of the existence of a particular item—search. The other element is the establishment of the need by the library—verify." For most libraries, verification is a redundancy. One can assume that the selector has, in the very process of selecting, established that a need exists for the particular book and has checked the library's holdings. Whatever terminology is used, however, searching/verification in too many libraries is carried to extremes and becomes a very costly waste of time. A few years ago I was asked to critique a manuscript that consisted of a number of libraries' acquisitions policies and procedures. One small college library reported that it had a book budget of $6,000 annually, and ordered 300 to 500 books each year (books were a lot cheaper then!). The policy stated that the staff consisted of one professional librarian and three clerical staff, "most of whose time is spent on searching and verification of titles." How silly can you get?

STEP 3: VENDOR ASSIGNMENT

Once the search has indicated that a title appears to be available, the acquisitions department must decide who will get the order. Will it go to a wholesaler? If so, which one? Will it be sent directly to the publisher? Will the book be picked up at a local retail bookstore, or ordered through the Internet? This discussion has been held at some length in Chapters 7 and 8, but a brief recap of the factors that should influence the assignment of a vendor is in order at this point.

These factors can be briefly summarized as the immediacy of the need for the book, its price, and the vendor's performance. If a book is a high-demand title, one that the public wants to read right now, the librarian may decide to send the order directly to the publisher, to order it from a local bookstore, or to transmit it to an online vendor via the Internet; one of the tradeoffs here, however, is that using these sources will, in most cases, mean that the cost of the book will be higher than it would be if the book were ordered from a major wholesaler. Plus, will you really get the book more slowly if the order is sent to a wholesaler? Considering the availability of online search and ordering capabilities, which means materials are shipped really quickly, the answer is probably no. Add to this the fact that the biggest wholesalers will indicate not only whether a book is in print but also their warehouse inventory of the title at the time you are ready to place an order, and it's hard to imagine that you'll get something faster from another kind of supplier, even at a higher price. A further advantage is that if you want to place an order for a hot title with wholesaler A and the book isn't in the warehouse, you can try wholesaler B's warehouse, and so on. But as always, if the order is going to be given to a wholesaler, the most important criterion for deciding which one is simply: Which one has given the library the best service at the best price with the greatest speed in the past?

STEP 4: PRODUCTION OF PURCHASE ORDERS

Depending on the size and sophistication of the library's acquisitions operation, the purchase order is typed, written manually, or, for many, if not most libraries today, entered as part of an automated process. The paper purchase order may be a single card or slip for each title ordered, or it may be a multititle order form. But whatever form it takes, the purchase order must include the following information:

- a unique purchase-order number. This enables the vendor to keep track of what has been shipped and how much the library owes for each shipment. It also enables the librarian to match shipments with materials ordered so as to approve invoices for payment.
- the library's full address. If books are to be shipped to another address, the "bill to" and "ship to" addresses should be clearly indicated.
- any specific terms that apply to the purchase order. For example, include instructions such as "Cancel titles not shipped within 90 days," "No back orders," and the like.
- complete information for each title ordered. This should give title, author, publisher, ISBN, price, edition, and number of copies or sets wanted.
- an authorized signature. This indicates that this is a valid purchase order.

If all this information is correct and clearly spelled out on the purchase order, the vendor should be able to provide the books with dispatch.

A word of caution is in order regarding one rather archaic purchase-order format. Sending a vendor a 3 x 5 slip for each title ordered is a thing of the past, especially in medium- and large-sized libraries, where thousands or tens of thousands of titles may be ordered each year. A few vendors still say they prefer the individual order slips, but one has to wonder what their operations are like, since someone has to handle and keep track of all those little slips of paper, filing and refiling and eventually unfiling them (if, of course, the vendor has been able to even find file cabinets that will hold such a size); it sounds almost Dickensian. Perhaps the money spent on this endless paper shuffling might better be saved and passed on to the vendor's library customers in the form of greater discounts. If a paper purchase order must be used, it's much wiser for the library to use a multiple-title form that can be sent in a letter-size, first-class envelope. The purchase-order form might also be a generic one that can be used for other library purchases besides books—a small economy but an economy nonetheless.

STEP 5: FUND ACCOUNTING

In most public libraries—at least those supported by tax dollars and/or operated under the aegis of a county government, city government, or school district—monies for purchase of library materials must be set aside to pay for the materials when they arrive. This process is called *encumbering* the funds. In other words, if the library sends out a purchase order for a new John Grisham novel priced at $28.95, that amount is reserved (encumbered) to pay for that book and cannot be used for anything else unless it is released, or *unencumbered*. Encumbered funds can only be unencumbered in two ways: when the book is received and paid for, or when the order is canceled by the vendor or the library. In most libraries, newly unencumbered funds are either charged to the unit of the library that ordered and received the book, or credited to that unit if the order is canceled.

All of this gives rise to the process called fund accounting, which is nothing more than keeping track of the funds encumbered and unencumbered for each of the library's units. In many small and medium-sized libraries this responsibility falls on the acquisitions department; in larger systems with data-processing capabilities and accounting departments, those units are usually responsible for fund accounting, although they depend on the acquisitions department for their data. In still other cases, libraries using a turnkey system such as DRA can have their fund accounting done by the system vendor, usually for a fee; can choose to have the capability for doing same programmed into the system so that the process can be done in-house; or can choose to add an acquisitions module that adds fund-accounting capability to their existing catalog/circulation system. Any one of the latter is far more efficient and cost-effective than using any form of manual fund accounting, a kind of drudgery that would do honor to Scrooge's firm. Still, many librarians persist in entering encumbrances and unencumbrances in just this way into ledgers or notebooks. There is no excuse for this. Even a simple program designed for an inexpensive personal computer or ready-made, low-cost business software can do all that work a lot more quickly and accurately than a legion of Bob Cratchits, and for a lot less money too. (An excellent report on the use of inexpensive generic business software to automate the acquisitions process appeared in the October 1998 issue of *Information Outlook*. In it the author describes how the Harold Kohn Vision Library at the State University of New York successfully modified a popular software accounting package to make the transition from manual ordering and fund accounting to a smooth and efficient automated process that saves the library both time and money, and that can easily be replicated by other libraries.)

There are several problems with the fund-accounting process, however, that have little to do with whether the accounting is done manually or some other way. One is that there are always going to be more monies encumbered than will actually be spent, and to the casual observer (or auditor!) it may appear that you are overspending; nevertheless, book prices should be encumbered at list (cover) price (since you're never actually certain exactly what the cost will be until the items arrive) and then adjusted when the invoice arrives. This is a somewhat tedious and time-consuming process, but is still better than trying to guess a final price at the time of encumbering and then turning around and doing it all over again when you finally determine the actual price you must pay.

In a sense, fund accounting is an exercise in futility; it is almost impossible for the librarian to know at any given time exactly what is owed and what will be left after the bills are paid, and the larger the library or system, the worse it is. For this reason, many libraries that must return any funds unspent at the end of the year to the library's governing agency clear the books toward the end of the fiscal year by canceling all orders not received by a certain date. This is a poor way of doing business for the library and makes it difficult for vendors as well, who potentially have to face an avalanche of cancellations as the cutoff date approaches, many of them for books that may have already been ordered for the library in good faith.

Why do fund accounting at all? Many librarians believe that it should be abolished because it is so inefficient and so costly a practice. But it seems likely that as long as library book funds are finite and have to be divided among the various units of the library, departments, branches, and all, the practice will continue for the foreseeable future.

STEP 6: RECEIPT OF MATERIALS

Within a few days or weeks or months, the materials will begin to arrive at the library. If the vendors who supply the materials are any good, packages will be clearly labeled with the purchase-order number noted on each carton so that it can be easily matched to the appropriate invoice and acquisitions record; the boxes will have withstood any crushing; an accurate packing list and invoice will be prominently attached and displayed on the outside of the carton—or, if inside the carton, on top of the material; and the number of cartons in the shipment will be clearly noted on *each* of the cartons within the shipment.

Anyone who has received book shipments, however, knows that Murphy's Law holds true here. Books are missing; cartons go astray; invoices never appear; packing lists are buried in books or under one of the bottom flaps of the carton; the U.S. Postal Service sends an empty carton or mailer, carefully shrink-wrapped on the outside with a notice saying, "Contents have been lost in transit"; books are crushed or watersoaked or damaged by oil or other liquids; the wrong books have been shipped; or the entire shipment should have gone to someone else. Book distribution can be as big a problem for libraries as it is for the producers of books (as discussed in Chapter 4), and is just as frustrating and costly for the customer as it is for the producers and distributors of books.

At any rate, the materials that have arrived need to be unpacked, sorted, checked against the packing slip/invoice, and matched up with the appropriate library record forms: order slips, request forms, database records, or whatever. The library must also verify that each book is the one ordered, and that the vendor has not made a mistake in edition, title, author, price, or other area. A brief physical examination of the book is in order here too: pages may be blank; the book may be printed upside down; sections of the book (signatures) may be transposed or missing; corners of the binding may be badly broken—anything could happen. If everything seems alright, the next step is to approve the invoice for payment.

STEP 7: INVOICE APPROVAL

If the right book is in hand at the right price and in the right condition, the stage is set for the next step—approving the invoice for payment and, in some automated libraries, automatically producing and issuing the check or voucher. Whatever the case, a careful check of the invoice is important. Was the correct number of books shipped, and is the price charged accurate based on the discount noted on the invoice? If so, the bill may be paid; if not, the library may have to make a claim, take a debit on the invoice, or return the book to the vendor for credit.

Most reliable vendors are more than willing to accept back defective or the wrong books if it was their fault—even if a few months have passed or the books have been processed. And to make it even easier, as mentioned in Chapter 9, some of the more enlightened vendors provide "instant-credit forms" to their customers. If there is a mistake in a shipment or on an invoice, the librarian only has to fill out one of these forms and mail it to the vendor, and credit for the amount will be immediately applied to the library's account, bypassing the whole tedious process of returning the book. Astute vendors realize that the cost of handling the return probably far exceeds the cost of the book, and it is easier and cheaper on both ends to avoid returns. Vendors often limit this perk to those librarians that they know can be trusted not to take advantage of this good thing, but then vendors *should* be able to trust all library book buyers.

Other vendors are not so enlightened; they insist that the librarian write for permission to return the book, fill out a special form to accompany the return, fill out a special mailing label, and send the book back before credit will be given or a replacement copy tendered. When you stop to think about it, that vendor has more than a lot of nerve, since it was the vendor's error that caused all this rigamarole to have to be done in the first place; a good librarian will not accept this kind of cavalier treatment, and will give the library's business to a vendor who has entered the twentieth century as far as ways of doing business go.

STEP 8: BAR CODING AND OTHER MISCELLANY

Libraries with automated circulation systems may have the acquisitions department attach bar codes for circulation purposes as the books are received. The department may also be responsible for stamping the books with ownership markings or attaching ownership labels, pockets (if catalog cards are still used), plastic jackets, "tattle-tape" antitheft strips, or other items. In larger libraries, books are more likely to be simply checked in and sent on to the catalog department, which will catalog them and then pass the books on to the processing department to do the work mentioned above. Still other libraries avoid the whole business by having the vendor provide the books with bar codes, jackets, labels, pockets, catalog cards, and "tattle-tapes." This type of service is particularly important to those libraries wanting books on their shelves in the minimum amount of time possible; as anyone who works in technical services knows, cataloging and processing—particularly the former—can take an inordinate amount of time, thus keeping the books off the shelves for weeks, months, even years. The cost of having books preprocessed is almost invariably cheaper than doing them in-house, and that too can be an important factor for budget-conscious libraries.

APPROVAL PLANS AND LEASING PLANS

APPROVAL PLANS

Approval plans are generally of three types: approval plans per se, blanket-order plans, and standing-order plans. These are often referred to as *gathering plans*. The first two are usually provided by wholesalers and the last by publishers, as a rule.

Under an *approval plan*, the librarian instructs a wholesaler to provide one copy of each new significant title in a given subject area or from a specific publisher's new releases. Restrictions can be imposed; for instance, no book above a certain price, no paperback editions, and the like. The better wholesalers ask the librarian to complete a detailed profile form in advance of the first shipment of approval books, which includes specifications and gives the vendor a firm idea of just what the library wants and doesn't want. When the approval books arrive, the librarian can then examine them and decide which to keep and which to return as "books not wanted" for full credit.

The *blanket-order plan* is one in which the librarian instructs the wholesaler to ship every new title in a specific area or from a specific publisher or publishers. Certain restrictions similar to those with approval plans may be imposed, but the titles sent under a blanket-order plan are *not* returnable.

Standing-order plans are usually provided by publishers rather than wholesalers. Under a standing-order plan, the librarian signs an agreement with a publisher to have one copy of every new title published or one copy each of titles from certain categories of the publisher's output, for example, all juvenile titles, no paperbacks, no titles over a certain price. Standing-order plan books are returnable for credit except for books acquired under a unique standing-order plan called the *Greenaway plan*. The books are supplied by the publisher just as customary standing-order plan books are, but because Greenaway plan books are heavily discounted (up to 70 percent in some cases) they are *never* returnable. It should be noted, however, that fewer and fewer publishers are offering Greenaway plans to libraries each year, and that those who still do offer them are continually decreasing the discount for such books.

Librarians use these gathering plans for several reasons. When book budgets increase but staff does not, there are fewer staff hours available for book selection. Librarians also cite the fact that changes in immigration patterns in the United States cause them to collect more books from foreign countries and in languages that may be unfamiliar to staff. Still others state that the increasing sophistication of library patrons has created demands for depth in the collection that did not exist a few decades ago and that many current selectors cannot handle. In university libraries, new curriculums may mean that books must be obtained on subjects unfamiliar to selection staff. Finally, there is the argument that in this age of smaller print runs, limited backlist, and books being declared out of print sooner than in past years, gathering plans can be one way to make sure the library gets new titles while they are still available.

But there are problems with gathering plans, too. Approval plans are costly to administer, both for the library and the vendor. A great deal of staff time is spent keeping records of all the books received while the decision is being made whether to keep or return them. Except under blanket-order plans, the books are rarely discounted; in fact, a surcharge is sometimes added to a book's price so that the vendor can make at least some profit. If a vendor does not scrupulously follow the library's requirements as noted in the profile, the library may find itself on the receiving end of a lot of books that are of marginal value, which means dealing with either a lot of returns immediately or doing a lot of weeding later on. (A splendid example of this is to be found in the experience of the State Library of Hawaii, which gave practically its entire budget to a major wholesaler in 1996 to select and supply *all* the books for the system. This action, which turned out to be a near catastrophe for that system as well as highly controversial in the broader library community, is discussed at some length in Chapter 12.) Conversely, if the vendor chooses not to send all the books the library may wish to examine, the collection may end up missing a lot of titles that really belong in it. Finally, the processes of budget allocations and fund accounting are made much more difficult when standing-order plans are used, for obvious reasons.

Approval plans are costly for vendors too, primarily because most libraries require only one copy of each new title for examination, and one-copy orders are never very profitable, especially when many of the single copies sent may be returned after six months or a year. Additionally, the very nature of the kinds of books a library contracts for under approval plans—such as technical, scientific, and professional books—means that they are the kind of books that the vendor may be able to get only at very short discount, so profit margins are smaller. Usually vendors have to do a substantial volume of approval-plan business to at least break even.

Not all the concerns of those opposed to approval plans have to do with their economic aspects, however; there are some philosophical problems as well. Collection development is a fundamental principle of librarianship, and intelligent selection of materials is a basic. Putting the selection process into the hands of a vendor who does not know the strengths and weaknesses of the collection is tantamount to abnegating the library's primary responsibility for selection and thus development—not just expansion—of the collection. If the vendor does not employ trained professionals—librarians—to choose the books sent to its customers, the library's collection may be weakened rather than strengthened. And even if the vendor does employ one or a few librarians to preselect the books for a given library's approval, it is hard to believe that these people have the enormous expertise required to make them experts in every field, especially those highly technical or otherwise arcane ones.

Many librarians believe that they became librarians to contribute to building organic and viable book collections; they resent the idea of turning their raison d'être for all those hours spent in library school over to a commercial operation whose primary goal is to make a profit. There are thus many valid reasons to seriously question the financial and philosophical ramifications of approval plans except for those institutions whose collecting is of such broad scope that the use of a few plans is warranted. For small and medium-sized libraries, however, using approval plans is questionable at best.

LEASE PLANS

Lease plans are useful for one purpose only, and that is to save the library from having to buy certain books. Leased books are usually titles that are likely to be in demand—a novel by a best-selling author, a mystery, a new self-help book on a subject of great current interest—but only for a relatively short time. Through this plan, the library may lease up to several dozen copies of a book and return them for partial credit once demand has lessened, perhaps keeping one or two copies for the permanent collection. The most well-known leasing plan, the McNaughton Plan, is operated by Brodart; a few other vendors attempted to come up with plans of their own, but found them too costly, too cumbersome, or both, and subsequently dropped them. (A handful of reference publishers, however, will not sell their books to libraries at all, but only lease them. Some, such as Rand-McNally, with its *Commercial Atlas*, go so far as to require that libraries return all old leased books before they can lease new ones—a costly and inefficient practice, to say the least.)

Many librarians feel that lease plans solve the problem of meeting public demand for ephemeral titles in a timely manner. The tradeoff, however, is that lease plans are much more costly than outright purchases both in terms of price per book and in administering the plans, which call for a huge amount of record keeping and a lot of unnecessary shipping, packaging, and handling costs.

A FEW FINAL NOTES

The book-ordering process is a complex one, but the steps involved are very simple and can be performed by clerical staff with a minimum of training if the operation is well thought out and each step planned, and if all steps in the various procedures are carefully monitored. For this reason, most acquisitions departments have few professional staff. The real problems, however, arise from the fact that even the professionals usually have little or no formal training in acquisitions work since few, if any, library schools offer courses in acquisitions, and those that do are primarily concerned with selecting books, not acquiring them.

The literature available on book ordering isn't much help, either. Too many tomes simply pass on antiquated and costly ways of doing things that have become traditional simply because they've always been done that way. For example, in his book *The Acquisition of Library Materials*, Stephen Ford devotes nearly 250 pages of numbing detail to discussing ways to perform the operations described in this chapter.

The tragedy is that librarians all over the United States are following procedures that in any other organization would result in either bankruptcy or wholesale firing of staff. And there is simply no excuse for it. Librarians must examine every single step of every single procedure to determine first, if it must be done this way, and second, why it must be done this way. In most cases, the answer to the first question will be "no," and to the second, "no good reason." It is up to us to come up with a better, faster, and less expensive way to provide better and faster service, and this is where the importance of at least a minimum level of automation becomes critical; options for automating the acquisitions process will be described in the next chapter, options that will help us follow one of Daniel Melcher's rules to live by when buying books: "Keeping the user constantly in mind is almost your only defense against sliding into procedures that perhaps make things easier for one clerk, but make things harder for your entire public. Eternal vigilance is the price of freedom from thoughtlessly burdensome procedures" (*Melcher on Acquisition*, p. 2).

11 AUTOMATION AND ACQUISITIONS

Imagine, if you will, a medium-sized library in a medium-sized American town a little more than a quarter of a century ago. It's a pleasant enough building on the outside, and the inside is just about the same: warm and welcoming, with shelves full of books beckoning to the steady stream of adults who come in to browse the fiction or to look something up in the reference collection or just to sit in one of the comfortable chairs near the tall windows and read a newspaper or magazine. Work tables await the after-school onslaught of teenagers with homework to do, and the children's librarian looks at the clock, noting that it's almost time for her charges too, full of energy now that they're free from school at last, and ready to find their favorite picture book or the newest Beverly Cleary. Within sight of everyone—patrons and staff alike—sits the ubiquitous card catalog, probably built of oak, with its many long drawers of spindled cards holding the key to everything that's in the library for those who are curious and intrepid enough to use it. At the nearby circulation desk, clerks wait to check in returned books and check out those that patrons have chosen. It all makes for a charming picture, all this that the patron sees—but behind the circulation desk, in that nether region labeled "Staff Only," lies another part of the library. It's the work room, and it's not a very pretty picture at all.

In precomputer days, the work room was the place where orders for books and magazines were produced (usually typed with carbons for needed extra copies) and readied for mailing; when books were received, they were unpacked, checked, and placed on trucks to be given to a cataloger. It was the cataloger's job to examine the books, decide what information needed to appear on the catalog cards, and, in some cases, type up the catalog card sets (some were even hand-written!) and see that they were filed properly in the public card catalog. Others in the work area used the cataloging information to produce ownership and other labels, and to record the Dewey number on the spine of each book—usually on typed labels that were glued on, but when necessary actually printed (gilded) on the spine. Still others examined the invoices for errors; if there were none, they then prepared the payment checks for vendors and mailed them or, if the invoices were not accurate, filed debits or claims for the discrepancies. All these routines done "behind closed doors" required a great deal of paperwork, and all that paper had to be filed, necessitating large numbers of bulky file cabinets that took up much of the space in the work room. In more enlightened libraries, the files were purged regularly, simply to make enough room to file new paperwork, but in some li-

113

braries the material was kept on file for years "just in case." Because all this work was done manually—with the typewriter as "state-of-the-art" automation—it was very tedious and very slow and thus required many staff members; as a result it took weeks or even months for new books to end up on the shelves in the public area for the use of patrons, even with a sizable staff working behind the scenes.

It took nearly twenty-five years for all this to change in libraries (in most of them, at least), and when the changes did occur they were almost always the result of automation, whether it was called by that term or not. The first change was somewhat subtle, but its later impact on all subsequent library automation was enormous. Led by Harriet Avram, the technical services director of the Library of Congress (LC), a group devised the MARC (Machine Readable Cataloging) format, a series of rules for coding cataloging data into a format that could be read by computers. LC, using the MARC rules, began printing catalog cards in the new format, which were soon purchased by thousands of libraries; later LC made MARC tapes available, which meant that libraries could produce and copy their own catalog cards. This had two major effects: first, the time spent cataloging in libraries could be cut back and used in other, better ways; and second, the use of the MARC format meant that all libraries had the same information in their catalogs, not just what individual catalogers might consider appropriate for their local catalogs. This latter factor, of course, made possible the development of such bibliographic utilities as OCLC, RLIN, and WLN in the United States, and ISM and AMICUS in Canada, among others, all of which built on and expanded LC's pioneering work.

State and regional networks soon followed, and cooperative resource sharing made online catalogs possible for any libraries that wanted them. As Kathleen Imhoff put it:

> Online catalogs proliferated among all sizes and types of libraries during the late 1970s and early 1980s. . . . Consortia and cooperative projects flourished . . . and stand-alone catalogs became online union catalogs available in many locations, the distance from the central catalog creation unit being of little consequence. Most libraries joined and participated in networks and cooperatives. During this time regional, state, and multistate networks were born. . . . The availability of bibliographic records in standard, machine-readable form was a key to unlocking the door to increased, easy, electronic resource sharing. Each state and region developed its own pace but by 1980 a large number of libraries had online catalogs. (Kathleen Imhoff, *Making the Most of New Technology*)

As a result, that workroom we visited earlier was a lot less cluttered with files and catalog-card stock, work tables, desks, and type-writers, and the cataloger's lot was, by and large, a much easier one. Also gone was that big, forbidding catalog in the public area of the library, replaced by computer terminals placed at a number of locations in the building for staff and patron use.

And what about the acquisitions process? Again, the standardization of bibliographic data indirectly began to lay the groundwork for automation of that costly and highly labor-intensive process also. By using MARC records, a library or library system created a database that could serve other purposes, especially creating purchase-order forms that could be hard copy (paper) or, later, transmitted via a modem to wholesalers—whose own databases were also created from MARC records. The fact that both library and vendor databases contained identical information made the processes of searching and verification easier for the library and more accurate, which cut down on the possibility of errors and thus cut costs for all concerned, both libraries and vendors. (For libraries who still needed catalog cards, the vendors that supplied them used MARC format, so even nonunion catalogs were more uniform than they had ever been in the past.) But few libraries saw this technology as having much to do with the acquisitions process.

As noted earlier, essentially all the routines performed in "behind-the-scenes" library operations—technical services functions—lend themselves beautifully to one degree of automation or another. As obvious as this may seem, few libraries, regardless of their size, automated those functions (other than those relating to cataloging and circulation) to the degree to which they could (and most likely should have) during the 1970s and much of the 1980s. By the beginning of the 1990s, however, most had begun to see the light.

In Chapter 10, I described the library acquisitions process as being on the surface a highly complex operation, but at base a series of extremely simple procedures. It is this very simplicity that makes the acquisitions process a prime target for automation; as libraries began to discover by the mid-1980s, virtually every one of the steps in that process can be done more efficiently in an automated environment than in a manual one. There are those who will argue that in small libraries, particularly, it is both simpler and more cost efficient to have a few clerks produce purchase orders and send them to vendors and receive the books and check them in and process them and check the bills and then pay them—and then turn around and do it all over again in a few days or a week or a month. Any rational analysis of the true cost of staff salaries, benefits, paid time off, and so on belies that assumption. It's not really simpler and cheaper to do things manually than to use automation; it's just more comfortable to do things the way they've always been done.

This is not to say that these libraries have to make enormous investments in the kind of high-tech gimmickry that has tended to monopolize booth space at library convention exhibits in recent years. Even the smallest library can save some of that staff cost by investing in an inexpensive personal computer with a modem and a few pieces of acquisitions software, which a number of wholesalers will be happy to provide gratis to their customers. The few hundred dollars the equipment will cost is a great deal less than the thousands of dollars it costs to pay just one clerk's salary and benefits for a year, even if the library is paying that person the minimum wage (heaven forbid!), and the savings can be used to purchase more materials or whatever else the library sees as a priority.

That alone should be enough to convince even the diehards among us to think long and hard about automating; but there is another, more subtle benefit that accrues to those who are considering whether to automate this part of the library's operations. Automating forces them to take a good look at just what the library is currently doing—the first step in improving anything—and then to ask some hard questions, questions that apply whether the library is just thinking about automating or starting to plan to improve or upgrade its automation. Some of those questions are:

- Why automate at all?
- What specific benefits do we hope to gain from automating or upgrading?
- Will these benefits contribute toward achieving the goals of the library, such as better service to users?
- How much will the process of automating cost? How will the library pay for it?
- Will the change to or in automation be achieved in-house or by outside consultants/vendors? If the latter, what kind of technical support will the vendor provide after the transition is completed?
- Who will train staff in the new procedures? How will work flow be maintained during the training and changeover periods?
- How will the library cope with the inevitable psychological problems and stress that staff will have in the face of major change?
- What hardware and software are available to meet the library's needs?
- What peripheral costs will automation require (new wiring, ergonomic furniture, mainframes, terminals, PCs, and the like)?
- How long will the changeover take?
- What experiences, problems, and successes have other libraries had during the changeover from manual to automated operations?

Once these questions have been raised and thoroughly discussed, the library is ready to move to the next step, which is looking at what equipment—hardware, software, peripherals—is out there and will best meet the needs of the institution. Those libraries that have not automated at all will have one set of needs. Those that are unable or unwilling to invest in very costly new equipment and/or sophisticated acquisitions programs will have another. Libraries that have already automated their cataloging and circulation and perhaps have a rudimentary automated, autonomous acquisitions system have yet another. Still, no matter what situation a library is in, there are really only three options:

1. an automated acquisitions system (software) provided by a wholesaler, usually free to its customers
2. a stand-alone system provided by a vendor or utility
3. a module that is part of a larger, multi-user system such as an automated circulation system or an online public access catalog—or both of these.

WHOLESALERS' SYSTEMS

The first step toward automating library acquisitions was taken by a vendor. More than twenty years ago, Ingram Book Company, a major full-line book wholesaler, offered retail booksellers and libraries its microfiche program. All you needed was a microfiche reader (which Ingram was willing to supply at nominal cost if you wished), and you had the key to searching tens of thousands of titles for availability and price. On a weekly or biweekly basis, for a very small fee, Ingram would send participating libraries two sets of microfiche containing listings of their warehouse, in-stock book inventory of several hundred thousand titles: one a listing by title, the other by author. The fiche contained lots of other valuable information too, such as publisher, publication date, edition/binding, ISBN, and price—including clearly spelled-out discount terms for any particular title—and Ingram's own title code, a six-digit number that simplified the ordering process. The fiche also helped the bookseller or librarian decide how many copies of a title to order by presenting information on best-seller listings, reviews in major media, special publisher promotions and advertising, author appearances, and movie or television tie-ins that were planned for the book. Best of all, however, since it might be assumed that a librarian who subscribed to Ingram's microfiche program intended to buy some books from that company, the fiche advised the buyer how many copies of a title were *in stock* in Ingram's four warehouses that week, or how many copies Ingram had *on order*, if it was not yet published. For those who used it, the Ingram microfiche proved to be a real boon, and as word of its usefulness spread at conferences and meetings, more and more libraries came to depend on it for ordering information that had been hard to come by in the past. The microfiche program, now containing information on some 450,000 titles, is still available to libraries that are not yet ready for online ordering or that simply wish to have it as a convenient search tool for staff or patrons.

Ingram's success with its pioneering use of microfiche soon led other wholesalers to try their hand at it. Baker & Taylor followed, joined later by a dozen smaller vendors, all of whom found the fiche to be a valuable marketing tool in selling books to libraries, which appreciated this inexpensive yet effective search tool. But even with the various fiche programs, those institutions still had to produce paper purchase orders to be mailed to the vendors manually or spend time on the telephone calling the nearest warehouse to place the orders. The vendors' answer was online ordering for those libraries that wanted to extend their "automation" beyond use of the fiche.

Their solution was a simple one. Libraries and bookstores could check out materials available from a vendor using either the microfiche or by searching the vendor database online; then, using a microcomputer or a PC and a piece of communications software (Pro-Comm was one of the first two-way communication tools used), the client could connect with the wholesaler's computer by modem and place the order. Ingram Book Company's free Flashback program, as it was called, was one example of early online ordering programs. Confirmation of orders placed using such programs usually followed within a few hours or—with the largest vendors, such as Ingram—instantly, with title-by-title, stock-status verification of all titles ordered; the confirmation report could then be printed out at the library to be used as an on-order record. Books ordered that were in stock at the vendor's warehouse were usually shipped with invoices within twenty-four hours of receipt of the order. It was, to say the least, light years beyond what libraries (and bookstores) had been doing from time immemorial, and by the mid-1980s it was the exception rather than the rule in book acquisitions, since the advantages were obvious enough to convince even the most stubborn that there really was a better way to buy books.

Today, Ingram, Baker & Taylor, and other wholesalers have refined their online ordering programs significantly. Ingram's Flashback gave way to Flashback II, which, like its predecessor, gave instant order confirmation and guaranteed maximum discounts to its users, and also interfaced with that company's primary search database, Ingram Books in Print on Disc; it allowed the customer to order only from Ingram Books, however. Flashback III, the latest version, offers all the benefits of Flashback II with the added advantages of, first, allowing the customer to send purchase orders either to Ingram or to a number of different vendors such as Baker & Taylor, and, second, giving the library a tool for creating management reports on such items as vendor performance and fill rates. Finally, Ingram's Web-based iPage provides for online searching of some 1.7 million titles from BIP, as well as online ordering from Ingram's 450,000 title inventory.

Baker & Taylor also offers free software for electronic ordering and inventory confirmation in its B&T Link program. Its latest and most sophisticated acquisitions program, TitleSource II, is comparable to Ingram's iPage, and like Ingram's product is user-site based. Libris2020, B&T's most sophisticated search-and-purchase system, is also available, but it is expensive; the cost for a three-concurrent-user license, for example, is approximately $15,000 exclusive of hardware. For the larger library system that requires extensive search capabilities, the ability to perform fund accounting, selection list preparation, vendor files and voucher preparation, online claiming, and an interface to bibliographic utilities, however, this Windows-based product may be well worth the cost. Brodart offers a free acquisitions program called PC Rose Plus to its customers and is developing a Web-based program to be known as Bibz.com that should be available in 2000. Other smaller vendors make online search-and-ordering services available to their customers as well, but their programs are not as encompassing or as sophisticated as those of the "giants" and have few of the "bells and whistles" that B&T's Libris 2020 or Ingram's iPage do. They are useful, nevertheless, and, as has been stated in this book a number of times, with some of the free programs and a personal computer or two, any library can order books so much more efficiently and economically than it can with even the leanest staff doing it all manually that it is almost criminal *not* to take advantage of the technology.

STAND-ALONE/NETWORK-BASED SYSTEMS AND MULTI-USER SYSTEM MODULES

A number of vendors offer total acquisitions programs that can be purchased or leased by the library, and others offer acquisitions modules—such as automated circulation and online public access catalogs—as optional parts of their total automated library systems. (The online catalogs often offer serials control modules to accompany the acquisitions modules, and a few systems do not sell one without the other.) It is safe to say that most libraries are more likely to purchase stand-alone programs based on PCs for two reasons. First, they are almost always much less expensive than modular systems: the programs themselves are cheaper, as is the equipment necessary for them; in addition, they don't require specialists to maintain the systems, heavy-duty wiring, extensive and ongoing training of staff, and so forth. Second, most stand-alone programs offer a full complement of the basic functions that libraries should expect in a fully automated system—not that much different from those offered by the modular programs, except for price and the intended purpose.

The thirteen basic acquisitions functions and capabilities that are common to both stand-alone and modular systems are the ability to:

1. download bibliographic records in full MARC format and retain that format
2. perform basic Boolean searches
3. access wholesalers' databases and download bibliographic records from them
4. order online from any vendor using a basic ordering standard (was BISAC, now EDIFACT), and claim online using the same standard
5. create and modify selection lists
6. create and maintain vendor files and vendor performance data reporting
7. use fund accounting
8. interface with a bibliographic utility or CD-ROM cataloging support systems for downloading bibliographic records
9. generate automatic notice of expiration of the library's cancellation period for outstanding orders and automatic claims
10. readily search check-in data for materials received
11. generate and prepare vouchers
12. produce hard-copy purchase orders for materials that cannot be ordered online

13. upgrade the system as improvements and enhancements are made available

In addition to the functions and capabilities listed above, for some libraries, particularly those with very large budgets for materials, multiple users, and complex ordering requirements, other desirable functions (available in most systems) include automatic currency conversion; in-depth management report generation; the ability to handle standing orders, approval plans, gifts and exchanges, and out-of-print want lists. The acquisitions modules for such systems are priced substantially higher than are modules for stand-alone and network-based systems.

Generally speaking, it is the size and complexity of the library system, as well as its budget, that determine which kind of automated acquisitions system it is willing to settle for. But whatever system a library chooses, it should offer everything the library needs at a competitive price with enough technical support to get it going and maintain it as necessary. (See Appendix B for a list of selected automated acquisitions vendors with brief descriptions of their products.)

12 PUBLISHING, BOOKS, AND ACQUISITIONS IN THE NEW MILLENNIUM

> That chaos has pervaded the book industry in the last three years is evident enough. Massive returns and the decline of independent booksellers are merely two symptoms of an industry searching to find itself, blurring formerly well-defined roles and redefining who does what.
> —Paul Hilts and James Lichtenberg,
> "Redefining Distribution"

> Perhaps it will be different in the next millennium, but the single word that best defined the bestseller game in the last decade of the 20th century was domination. In 1997, the merger news involved Penguin and Putnam; in 1998, the big merger was the combination of Random House and Bantam Doubleday Dell; and last year [1999] it was HarperCollins' takeover of Morrow and Avon. That means that, each year, even fewer corporations control the weekly bestseller charts.
> —Daisy Maryles,
> "Connecting the Numbers"

PUBLISHING, BOOKS, AND BOOK DISTRIBUTION

To describe the last three decades of the book-publishing industry, especially its trade book-publishing arm, as having been chaotic is an understatement of the first order. The industry mania for acquisitions and mergers showed no signs of abating; respected and important publishers bowed to the economic pressures of the industry and bit the dust; and blockbuster books got more attention than ever before. A huge number of titles are still being published each year (more than 60,000 in 1999) even though initial print runs continue to get smaller, the in-print lives of the most titles get shorter and shorter, and book prices increase steadily.

Edwin McDowell, a writer on publishing for the *New York Times*, called his September 19, 1988, column in that newspaper "Never Have So Few Published for So Many." In it he noted Random House's surprise acquisition of two of the few remaining privately owned publishing houses, Crown Publishers and Vanguard Press; only a few years later, Random was itself the victim of a surprise acquisition by Advance Publications, a private holding company owned by the Newhouse family of newspaper ownership fame. But there was more to come for this august publishing company; in 1998, the publishing world was stunned when Random was bought for an estimated $1.4 billion from the Newhouses by Bertelsmann, which already owned Bantam Doubleday Dell, making the German company the industry leader in American trade-book publishing.

In a parallel development in nontrade publishing, Viacom, the owner of Simon & Schuster, decided to split out the company's educational, professional/business, and reference divisions and offer them for sale. The buyer was British conglomerate Pearson PLC, which forced a $4.6 billion deal that made Pearson one of the four major American publishers of professional and reference books. Thus, the merger and takeover mania of the 1990s was not limited to trade publishers but spread across the whole spectrum of the book-publishing industry.

Consolidation is not always a bad thing, of course, but it does have consequences for library book buyers. One is that the new owners are often companies with no real commitment to book publishing per se, and they look on it as just another means of making a profit; the bottom line is what counts. Ergo, the never-ending search for the blockbuster title intensifies at the expense of many midlist titles, which libraries buy a very large percentage of (as well as backlist). It is common knowledge in the publishing industry that about 2 percent of the nation's publishers produce 75 percent of its trade books, and furthermore that the top 30 percent of trade publishers are responsible for 99 percent of the trade books published in this country. So, logically enough, as this control of a huge percentage of the books of general interest published today narrows, and as more trade publishers sacrifice midlist and backlist titles on the altar of the blockbuster, the variety among trade books from which librarians can choose also narrows. Maxwell Lillienstein, general counsel for the American Booksellers Association, wrote in the association's trade journal a decade ago that "as a result of recent acquisitions, the four largest American publishers . . . now account for sales of 27 percent of domestic and export sales of *all books of all types*. The top 12 publishers account for an equally staggering 56 percent of all such sales"—and this was years before the monumental mergers mentioned above; the only thing that has really changed is that the names at the top are a bit different. Some further startling figures that relate to consolidation as well as to blockbusters appeared in *Publishers Weekly* on January 10, 2000: "One megagroup—Random House Inc.—alone accounts for almost 40% of all hardcover bestsellers and one-third of all paperback bestsellers. Add five more corporations . . . and you have 10 firms occupying about 95% of all hardcover bestseller positions. . . . So much in the hands of so few has been the story for most of the '90s" (Maryles, 2000: 25). What is clear is that fewer and fewer companies control more and more of what is published for the general reader in this country, and that has implications for anyone who is interested in books.

The irony of it all is that while the best-sellers are pretty much controlled by a handful of trade publishing companies, an increasing percentage of midlist books, a group extremely important to libraries, are coming from small, independent, and sometimes esoteric publishers who are, in many cases, taking up the slack in trade publishing. The problem for library book buyers is that these titles are sometimes hard to find; many of these companies' titles are not widely advertised, nor are they reviewed with any regularity in the usual library review media. While it should be noted here that the situation *has* improved a great deal in this regard over the last decade, there are and probably always will be thousands of titles that may be important to libraries but will never appear on library shelves because reviews of them were not available for selectors.

This is not surprising; consider that each of the four major review journals used by most libraries (*Library Journal*, *Kirkus Reviews*, *Booklist*, and *Publishers Weekly*) reviews only between 2,000 and 5,000 titles per year—out of the more than 60,000 published—and that there is great overlap among the titles reviewed. It is clear that these review media, through no fault of their own, face becoming increasingly inadequate as tools for solid collection building in spite of solid efforts on their part to cover as much of the independent presses' output as they can; however, the problem remains that there is only so much space available in each journal for reviews. Yet a recent article in *Library Journal* by its book review editor, Francine Fialkoff, noted that an *LJ* survey in 1998 revealed that 96 percent of librarians surveyed cited reviews as an essential tool for purchasing decisions. Perhaps it is time for librarians to take another look at this long-standing dependence on the review media and dare to take some risks. This idea is reinforced by the fact that most people in the book business believe that the economics of publishing, particularly the ongoing problem of returns by booksellers and wholesalers, will continue to mandate shorter initial and subsequent print runs, and that books will continue to go out of stock and out of print more rapidly than ever before. As a result, librarians responsible for both selection and acquisition of books will be forced to do so a lot faster than they have in the past, or else too many books will be gone long before either the selection decision is made or the acquisitions process begins, or both, which certainly will be a major factor in any realistic collection development planning.

IMPLICATIONS FOR ACQUISITIONS

Selecting and ordering more quickly may not be quite as simple as it sounds, however. Some American libraries may have to totally revamp many processes and procedures that have been in place for years and that consequently have become both sacrosanct and comfortable—in spite of the fact that they are highly likely to be both cost and labor intensive and inefficient to boot. Others may need to set up regularly scheduled, periodic, serious cost/time studies of the entire acquisitions process, especially if the library is to continue to upgrade the automated acquisitions program it is already using. Finally, libraries may face a sizable initial outlay of funds to pay for the equipment and training required to make necessary changes, as well as budgeting for future improvements.

Of course, none of this will be easy, and none of it will make staff members very happy, whether it is making the initial move into automation or dealing with the idea that the library will likely continue to make change an ongoing policy in order to meet future needs. Resistance to change, particularly changes in hallowed and comfortable routines, can be considered a given and is a factor that must be planned for in any restructuring process. Two things must be kept in mind as the process begins, however: the first is the library's goal or goals as an organization; the second is that the library that wishes to achieve such a goal or goals can sometimes be at the mercy of trends and events over which it has little, if any, control, such as changes in the publishing industry or capricious library governing and funding agencies. But if the library's primary goal is excellence in service to its patron community, then learning to deal with these trends and events is the only way possible to meet that goal. The first step in doing this is to define the problem, and the next is to take necessary steps to solve it.

This first step—defining the problem—in many public libraries is easy: books take too long to get onto the library's shelves because the library does too many things in ways that are not necessarily best, but simply how they have always been done. Let's look at a few of these time-honored, often sacrosanct procedures:

- waiting for reviews
- the use of gathering plans
- the paper monster
- the Buckram Syndrome

WAITING FOR REVIEWS

Many librarians will not order a book until one, two, three, or even more reviews of the book have appeared. This is, to put it bluntly, madness, for two reasons. First, a large majority of books published are never reviewed anywhere, which limits the pool from which to choose books. Second, these librarians could safely order most of the books they want without ever seeing a review, since most of the books they order are trade books published by tried-and-true publishers of decent writers' works. Why should you have to wait for a review of a new Mary Higgins Clark novel, a new Mobil Guide, a new Beverly Cleary romp for children or a Richard Peck novel for young adults, for example? The answer is, of course, you shouldn't.

USING GATHERING PLANS

Gathering plans are probably the most time-consuming, costly, and inefficient methods of generating and processing book orders ever invented. It can (and usually does) take months from the receipt and examination of approval books, to the manual creation of a buying list, to choosing and verifying titles wanted by branches, to collating order lists, to producing and sending purchase orders, to performing initial steps in the fund-accounting process. Chances are great that by the time the order reaches the vendor, a large percentage of the books ordered will no longer be available: they'll be OP or OS. When the staff time needed to administer the gathering plans is factored in, this becomes an even more costly way to obtain books. Someone has to keep track of all those books the vendor has sent for examination: get them to and from the appropriate selectors, assign the ones wanted to the appropriate agency, return the books that are not wanted, and all the while shuffle those piles of papers that go along with each step. The question then becomes, why have these plans at all? If what separates the librarian from the bookstore owner is the librarian's training and ability to select books to build an organic, dynamic, vital collection, why abrogate that crucial function and hand it over to a commercial vendor? Why bother to hire professional librarians if someone else is going to perform one of their basic professional functions? Save some money and hire a few clerks instead. Approval plans, except for the largest university and research libraries, are a waste of time, money, and professional training and skills.

TAMING THE PAPER MONSTER

Walk into the acquisitions department of a lot of libraries today, and you'll see that two items of furniture predominate—file cabinets and desks. The file cabinets are necessary to hold the thousands of paper records that staff must sort, resort, and sometimes unsort; the desks are necessary to hold the staff who perform these often unnecessary tasks. Anyone who has ever tried to modernize operations by eliminating some of these files knows that it is an uphill battle; staff want to hold on to that sixth copy of a purchase order "just in case"—even though one of the other equally unnecessary copies would work just as well. Or staff feel that all those pieces of paper should be held on file in perpetuity, "just in case" someone questions a transaction five or ten or twenty years in the future. In too many cases, libraries make too many copies of every form used, spend too much time and money filing and maintaining them, and keep them filed away for too long. If the vast majority of order transactions are not cleared within six months, then something is wrong with the order process; if they *are* cleared, then why keep files on them? Even given a worst-case scenario, if "just in case" ever comes true, it will happen rarely enough so that no one should have any scruples about regular and frequent purging of files.

But, you are probably thinking, most libraries *are* automated today. As a matter of fact, this is a little true but also a little false. The libraries that have automated certain functions have by and large limited this to either the catalog/cataloging, circulation, or both—but relatively few have automated the acquisitions function. Richard W. Boss, in a 1997 study of libraries' use of automated acquisitions systems, found that

> acquisitions and serials control are now part of almost all multi-user automated system products and a number of microcomputer-based systems, those running on IBM and compatible personal computers, or Macintosh products, yet a minority of libraries have implemented these modules as part of their integrated library systems . . . [and] vendors of micro-based products quote figures for both modules [acquisitions and serials control] of fewer than 10 percent of their customers. (Boss, 1997: 456)

For most public libraries especially, the closest they have come to automated acquisitions is the use of vendor-provided software of one kind or another, which is probably all that a lot of them need. Whether this will remain the case, however, remains to be seen as new media and new technology require new techniques, software, and equipment, just as occurred in the late 1970s, when libraries got tired of buying MARC-format catalog cards and decided to go for tapes they could download. The point is clear. No matter how much you love your 3x5 order slips and fund-accounting ledgers, or your Ingram or B&T microfiche, remember the words of Robert Frost: "Nothing gold can stay"—but who'd want it to anyway, if it's a hoary old anachronism?

CONQUERING THE BUCKRAM SYNDROME

Writing three decades ago in her monograph, *The Buckram Syndrome* (American Library Association, 1968), Marie T. Curley reported on a survey conducted among 3,200 public libraries in the United States that attempted to evaluate libraries' attitudes toward the purchase and use of paperbacks in their collections. To quote Ms. Curley,

> The very first impression which emerged from a casual study of the questionnaires was decidedly negative. It revealed beyond the shadow of a doubt that, even now [in 1965, when the survey was taken], when the paperback revolution is having a dramatic impact on the reading public who are actual and potential library users, our public libraries for the most part have not even begun to utilize this force for valid library purposes. (Curley, 1968: 5–6)

Sadly, Curley's comments are virtually as valid today for libraries as they were thirty-five years ago. Too many librarians still seem just as convinced in the year 2000 that any book really worth its literary salt has a hard cover, and that paperbacks, particularly mass market but too often trade also, are somehow inferior. These opinions are based on a few myths that need dispelling:

1. *Paperbacks don't hold up.* Actually, the state of paperback binding technology appears to be a lot more advanced than that of hardcover. I have seen a Harlequin paperback romance remain intact (albeit a little shopworn) after thirty-seven circulations, while almost every copy of a $28 hardcover bestseller of 1998 had two or more signatures fall out after two circulations. It's a lot easier and cheaper to replace a defective copy of a trade or mass-market paperback than a hardcover book, which ought to tell us something.
2. *The reading public does not like paperbacks.* Sure. That's why the nation's drugstores, supermarkets, airports, discount stores, chain bookstores, ad infinitum, stock them by the thousands. For some of the reading public, paperback is the format of choice; young adult readers frequently will not read the hardcover of even their favorite author's work, preferring to wait until the paperback comes out. Children's series books, such as the Boxcar Children and Goosebumps series, are sold only in paper, and were a real sales phenomenon of the 1990s. When

thinking about those hardbacks so many love, it's wise to remember that the possibility of paperback reprint rights is a major factor in the decision of whether a publisher will produce any trade book in hardcover, as well as being a financial boon to the book's author. In short, it's only some librarians who suffer from the syndrome, but in light of today's publishing and financial realities, it's time to seek a cure.

3. *Paperback books are hard to get.* This may once have been true, but certainly isn't any more. In the past, many mass-market paperback publishers refused to sell their products directly to libraries, so library customers had to go to independent distributors for them. For the last thirty years, however, a number of wholesalers have specialized in distributing them to libraries and schools. The Educational Paperback Association has encouraged these vendors, so today nearly all general, full-line wholesalers stock almost all mass-market paperback titles as well as trade paperbacks and supply them to their library customers quickly and at very reasonable cost.

4. *Paperback books just aren't as "respectable" as hardcovers.* This is about as silly an argument as you can get, since the vast majority of paperbacks started out as hardcovers in the first place. But a classic example of library paperback snobbery goes back a number of years, when a writer named John D. McDonald had a string of novels published in paperback starring a certain private eye, Travis McGee. The series was wildly successful, and enjoyed by readers at all levels. Libraries would not buy the books, however, because they had been published as paperback originals. Aye, but here's the rub: suddenly, a decade or so after the series started to run, a major trade publisher, Lippincott, noting the huge success of these paperback novels, began to reissue each book in the series in hardcover; just as suddenly Travis McGee books became respectable enough for libraries to purchase.

The truth about buying paperbacks for libraries today is that paperbacks, whether mass market or trade/quality, are less expensive and more available than hardcovers. It costs less to buy them initially, and it costs less to replace missing or worn-out copies. They are more available simply because paperback printings are usually much bigger than hardcover printings. And even when simultaneous hardcover/paperback editions are released, the printing of the latter edition will still be many times greater than the hardcover printing. In short, if you can't get your orders out fast enough to get the hardcover before it goes OP or OS, you really can settle for the paperback—and just may have to if you want the book at all.

There's one final argument for paperbacks: Which would you prefer to weed, a shelf of year-old hardcover copies of Stephen King's last best-seller, for which you paid $32.00 per copy, or a shelf with two hardcovers of the title and the rest paperbacks that cost you less than $7.00 each after your discount?

ACQUISITIONS AND ISSUES FOR THE NEXT DECADE

Above and beyond all the issues that have been discussed in this book, several more arose at the close of the twentieth century that will certainly have some implications for library book purchasing in the year 2000 and beyond. One of the most critical of these is the issue of outsourcing.

Outsourcing refers to the practice of handing over certain library functions to a company in the private sector. This is certainly not new; many libraries contract with wholesalers to catalog, process, and label their books, while others use vendors to do some or even most of their book selection through gathering plans such as approval plans. But in the mid-1990s, outsourcing was carried to an extreme that surprised and shocked most of the library world, not just because of the process itself but because of what ensued as a result of it.

The Hawaii State Public Library System is comprised of forty-eight branches located throughout the state. In the past, selection was done by library staff, and purchasing of books was done through the same channels used by most other libraries—publishers, wholesalers, and some others. To cut costs, the State Librarian of Hawaii in 1996 offered up *all* the system's business to the bidder who submitted the best price and the highest discount. The vendor who got the contract was also to do all processing and cataloging of the books, and would do all the selection of materials for the system; in return the vendor would be paid a flat rate per book, regardless of its list price, and would be guaranteed that no books would be returned to the vendor. The three largest wholesalers, Baker & Taylor, Ingram Books, and Brodart all bid on the contract, and the eventual winner was Baker & Taylor (B&T). As a result, B&T was given a contract to supply all books to the Hawaiian system for five and a half years at a total cost of $11.2 million, based on B&T's cost to the library of $20.94 per book.

Before many months had passed, complaints from the branches began to be heard. Those who had once had a hand in selection were disgruntled to have lost that part of their jobs (which is where the economy was to come in, since the administration felt it would have more staff hours for public service that way), but almost all staff complained of what they were getting from B&T—and, even more importantly, what they were *not* getting. The children's librarians, for example, complained that they were receiving hundreds of cheap series paperbacks (at $20.94 a crack!) and little else. Practically no books of local interest were received, and hardcovers of all kinds dribbled in slowly at best. Duplicate copies of titles of little interest were the rule, and pricier books—such as professional, art, and reference—were severely limited.

As complaints mounted and began to reach the pages of the library press and the Internet library listservs, B&T went on the defensive, claiming that it was doing exactly what had been promised, and that any problems that had occurred were a result of the poor branch book needs profiles given to them by the library system, but to little avail. The uproar became so great that in 1997 the U.S. Justice Department entered the investigation and began looking into the charges that not only had the wholesaler failed to meet its obligations to the Hawaii State Library, but also, as reported in *Library Journal*'s March 1, 1997 issue, was alleged to have engaged in the practice of "systematically short-discounting libraries since 1979." A year later, the library system's director was fired, the contract with B&T was canceled by the State of Hawaii, and selection and acquisitions were subsequently returned to the library staff. As has been mentioned in this book many times, there is no substitute for continuing and careful evaluation of vendor performance if the library is to get its money's worth, and there can be dire consequences when the vendor is allowed to call the shots, especially in a bid situation, as happened in Hawaii. The American Library Association, after much debate, created a task force to look into the whole outsourcing question, but has been unable to resolve the issue; a number of states—including Florida, Ohio, and at least fifteen others—started their own investigations of this particular wholesaler's practices, but the lesson is clear: *caveat emptor*—let the buyer beware!

A second issue that will certainly have an effect on libraries and will undoubtedly be felt in the area of acquisitions sooner or later is the whole phenomenon of electronic retailing. As book retailers on the Internet continue to expand their sales and services, it is logical to see libraries as a potential market. Amazon.com, for example, has already worked out a simple method of electronic searching of its database and ordering with a few libraries; it requires no sophisticated equipment and even offers a discount, no less (although the discount can be eaten up by shipping-and-handling charges on smaller orders). As Karen G. Schneider wrote in *American Libraries*, "the Web is rapidly changing how we do collection development, and the availability of online bookstores—the poor librarian's *Books in Print*—is just the beginning. Dire warnings about the quality of data on Amazon.com or barnes&noble.com wear a little thin when you consider the price [free]. . . . And . . . 'Amazon' is easy on the eyes—the format is really user-friendly" (Schneider, 1999: 100). There may be a long way to go, but it's not hard to believe that sooner or later online retailers will figure out a way to meet the needs of libraries just as they have the needs of the millions of customers they have been serving over the last few years; it will be up to acquisitions librarians to learn to deal with another aspect of automation as part of the whole acquisitions process.

A final challenge to acquisitions librarians has just begun to be noticed by the library world. As this book was being written, Scribner's published Stephen King's most recent novel, *Riding the Bullet*, as an online-only book—an "e-book" (a book whose content is distributed electronically) that could be read on a computer screen at home or downloaded to one of the many dedicated-reader, digital devices that are already on the market (such as Palm Pilot, Rocket, NetLibrary, NetBooks, Microsoft's Clear Type). Depending on your equipment, the "book" was either free (if downloaded from Amazon.com) for reading or cost a nominal amount ($2.50), but there was a slight catch; the file was encrypted so that it could be read only on the device that downloaded it and could not be printed, but no one seemed to mind that. One problem for libraries is obvious: How do you circulate an e-book that you've downloaded if it's so encrypted? And, in an era where libraries are increasingly expected to deliver their services and their "goods" directly to patrons' home computers, how will they manage to do this with encrypted e-books? But there are many other questions that will have to be answered as the e-book becomes more common: What kind of equipment will be needed to support text in this format? How will it be ordered? How does the library catalog it, shelve it, circulate it, and on and on? For the time being, these are somewhat academic questions, but librarians must remember that King's book is not an isolated phenomenon; there are already nearly 20,000 titles available as e-books from just the four largest e-book publishers (FatBrain, Peanut, NuvoMedia, and NetLibrary). And, if anyone doubts that the e-book is here to stay, Nora Rawlinson, editor of *Library Journal*, announced early in 2000 that her journal will begin featuring a regular column highlighting the business of e-publishing and e-books. From all appearances, the brave new world is already upon us and here to stay; let the (library) buyer beware.

THE SUCCESSFUL ACQUISITIONS LIBRARIAN IN THE TWENTY-FIRST CENTURY

None of the problems discussed here will be easily solved, and all will undoubtedly require some fundamental rethinking of our roles and responsibilities as acquisitions librarians. What must the acquisitions librarian of the year 2000 and beyond be like?

First, the person charged with the acquisition of books must be fully committed to supporting the library's mission and attaining its goals. The acquisitions librarian will not regard the acquisitions department and its work as an end unto itself nor allow it to become nothing more than a part of that exotic, insular little fiefdom that has come to exist in too many libraries—the Technical Services Department. Instead, the acquisitions librarian will be an integral part of the entire library's program of service to its patrons, and will insist that acquisitions staff members always keep the larger goals of the library in mind as they perform their functions.

The acquisitions librarian of the future will be both critical of existing procedures and receptive to new ideas. The questions that must constantly be asked are: Why are we doing it this way? How can we do it better? If the answer lies in automating a procedure or a whole set of procedures, then the good acquisitions librarian will not only attempt to overcome Luddite fears of new technology but also learn what is available to make the library more cost and dollar efficient— and at the same time help and inspire staff in dealing constructively with the changes that automation inevitably brings.

Acquisitions librarians constantly will be aware of the changes in publishing and book distribution that impact on the acquisitions process and will devise ways of coping with them. They will read the journals that monitor these changes, such as *Publishers Weekly* and *Library Journal*, and will communicate what these changes may mean to their colleagues in other areas of service in the library. They will also attempt to influence the course of more deleterious changes in those industries through communicating the library's needs firmly and clearly to publishers, vendors, and their professional associations. And they won't hesitate to call to task those who abuse the good faith of their dealings with the library.

For many now working in acquisitions this may be a challenge; for some it may even be impossible. But if libraries of the future are to be well served and their users provided with the excellence in library service to which they are entitled, then the challenges *must* be met, however difficult they are. Who knows, it may even prove to be fun!

APPENDIX A: SELECTED U.S. BOOK WHOLESALERS

Wholesalers listed below are primarily full-line vendors, with some specialized jobbers included. None of them drop ship; all maintain substantial warehouse inventories, and all have been in business for a long time. Special services offered are noted, as are electronic ordering capability, e-mail addresses, and Website addresses (when available). For a more complete listing, see *Literary Market Place*.

Academic Book Center, Inc.
5600 N.E. Hassalo Street
Portland, OR 97213
e-mail: *info@acbc.com*
Website: www.acbc.com
Full service jobber; approval plans, standing-order service.

Adler's Foreign Books
8220 Christiana Avenue
Skokie, IL 60076
e-mail: *alice@mepnet.com*
Specializes in books from Western European and Latin American publishers.

Ambassador Book Service, Inc.
42 Chasner Street
Hempstead, NY 11550
e-mail: *abs@class.org*
Website: www.absbook.com
Scientific, technical, and professional books; standing-order plans, approval plans, electronic ordering.

Baker & Taylor Books
2709 Water Ridge Parkway
Charlotte, NC 28217
e-mail: *btinfo@baker-taylor.e-mail.com*
Website: baker-taylor.com
Full-line jobber; approval and standing-order plans; processing; catalog cards; electronic ordering.

Ballen Booksellers International, Inc.
66 Austin Boulevard
Commack, NY 11725
Specializes in scientific, technical, professional, and university-press
books; offers continuation, standing-order, and approval plans.

Bilingual Publications Company
270 Lafayette Street, Suite 705
New York, NY 10012
e-mail: *lindagoodman@juno.com*
Imports and distributes books and audiocassettes in Spanish, including juveniles; carries contemporary Latin American fiction.

Blackwell's Book Services (formerly Blackwell North America)
6024 S.W. Jean Road, Building G
Lake Oswego, OR 97035
e-mail: *bridges@bname.blackwell.com*
Supplies scientific, scholarly, professional, technical, university press books; provides approval and standing-order plans, electronic ordering.

The Book House, Inc.
208 West Chicago Street
Jonesville, MI 49250
e-mail: *bhinfo@thebookhouse.com*
Website: www.thebookhouse.com
Full-line jobber; claims to be able to provide any book in print, which is, of course, impossible; electronic ordering.

Book Wholesalers, Inc.
1847 Mercer Road
Lexington, KY 40511
Specializes in children's books and audiovisual material; standing-order plans, electronic ordering.

Bookazine Company, Inc.
75 Hook Road
Bayonne, NJ 07002
Full-line wholesaler; specializes in books of Jewish and African American interest.

The Bookmen, Inc.
525 North Third Street
Minneapolis, MN 55401
Complete book wholesaler, but specializes in paperbacks.

Bookpeople Employee's Association Inc. (formerly Bookpeople Inc.)
7900 Edgewater Drive
Oakland, CA 94621
Website: bponline.com
Full-line wholesaler; handles small press titles.

Bound to Stay Bound Books, Inc.
1880 West Morton Road
Jacksonville, IL 62650
Website: www.btsbooks.com
Specializes in prebound juvenile books.

Brodart Company
500 Arch Street
Williamsport, PA 17705
e-mail: *bookinfo@brodart.com*
Full-line wholesaler; provides catalog cards, fully processed books, and
    McNaughton leasing plan.

China Books & Periodicals, Inc.
2929 24th Street
San Francisco, CA 94110
e-mail: *info@chinabooks.com*
Website: chinabooks.com
Distributes books by, about, and from China.

Christian Book Distributors, Inc.
Box 6000
140 Summit Street
Peabody MA 01961–6000
Website: www.chrbook.com
Religious reference, language, popular, bibles, juveniles, videos, and
    other.

Coutts Library Service, Inc.
1823 Maryland Avenue
Niagara Falls, NY 14302–1000
e-mail: *coutts@wizbang.coutts.on.ca*
Provides books of all publishers; offers continuation and approval
    plans, electronic ordering.

The Distributors
702 S. Michigan
South Bend, IN 46601
e-mail: *info@thedistributors.com*
Website: thedistributors.com
Large warehouse inventory of small press titles; electronic ordering.

The Edu-Tech Corporation
65 Bailey Road
Fairfield, CT 06432
Specializes in remainders of interest to libraries; audio- and videocas-
    settes.

Emery-Pratt Company
1966 West Main Street
Owosso, MI 48867
e-mail: *custserv@emery-pratt.com*
Website: emery-pratt.com
Full-line wholesaler; offers cataloged books, standing-order plan, elec-
    tronic ordering.

European Book Company, Inc.
925 Larkin Street
San Francisco, CA 94109
e-mail: *europeanbk@aol.com*
Specializes in foreign-language materials.

Follett Library Resources
4506 Northwest Highway
Crystal Lake, IL 60014
Full-line wholesaler specializing in juveniles; catalog cards and full
    processing available.

French & European Publications, Inc.
Rockefeller Center Promenade
610 Fifth Avenue
New York, NY 10020
Website: frencheuropean.com
Specializes in French and Spanish books, textbooks, and dictionaries.

Hotho & Company
Box 9738
8916 Norwood Street
Fort Worth, TX 76147–2738
Remainders; offers catalog cards and kits, approval plan, audio-visual material.

Ingram Book Company
One Ingram Boulevard
La Vergne, TN 37086–1986
Website: www.ingrambook.com
Full-line wholesaler; electronic ordering; all services.

Koen Book Distributors, Inc.
10 Twosome Drive
Moorestown, NJ 08057
e-mail: *kbdinfo@koen.com*
Website: www.koen.com
Full-line wholesaler.

Midwest Library Service
11443 St. Charles Rock Road
Bridgeton, MO 63044
e-mail: *mail@midwestls.com*
Scientific, technical, medical, trade books.

Partners Book Distributing Inc.
2325 Jarco Drive
Holt, MI 48842
National distributor of small press materials.

Quality Books, Inc.
1003 W. Pines Road
Oregon, IL 61061
e-mail: *qualitybooks@dawson.com*
Specializes in small press titles, remainders of interest to libraries; electronic ordering.

Samuel Weiser Inc.
PO Box 612
York Beach, ME 03910–0612
e-mail: *weiserbooks@worldnet.art.net*
Alternative healing, new age, Eastern philosophy, and similar.

Spring Arbor Distributors
10885 Textile Road
Belleville, MI 48111
Christian books, music, videos, bibles.

Sundance Publishers & Distributors, Inc.
Box 1326
Newtown Road
Littleton, MS 01460
e-mail: *info@sundancepub.com*
Website: www.sundancepub.com
Specializes in paperbacks for libraries.

Unique Books, Inc.
4230 Grove Avenue
Gurnee, IL 60031
Specializes in small press titles.

Yankee Book Peddler, Inc. (merged with Baker & Taylor in 1999)
999 Maple Street
Contoocook, NH 03229
Full-line wholesaler; offers standing-order and approval plans.

APPENDIX B:
SELECTED AUTOMATED ACQUISITIONS SYSTEMS

A number of tools for automating the acquisitions process are available for libraries. The most inexpensive and often the most practical for small and medium-sized libraries are those provided by wholesalers, as described in Chapter 11. But for libraries that wish to unify the acquisitions process with other automated library functions—such as an online public-access catalog, circulation, and/or serials control—certain vendors provide acquisitions programs or modules that can be easily integrated into the library's other functions and that can interface with library materials' vendors databases for ordering purposes, among other things. A dozen of the most popular of them are listed here, with brief data about each. Web addresses are also given; many of these vendors provide demos of their system for anyone who wants to log on, and this can be very informative. (It should be noted that there are many other automated systems vendors, but not all have acquisitions subsystems and so are not listed here.)

Ameritech Library Services: See **epixtech**

Best Seller, Inc.
3300 Cote Vertu, Suite 203
Montreal, Quebec
Canada H4R 2B7
Website: www.bestseller.com
Not yet very well known in the United States, this vendor aims its
  product, the Portfolio system (available as a turnkey or software-
  only program), at the larger library. Its acquisitions module has
  everything such a library might ask for: detailed searching, currency conversion, customized forms design, depository management, supplier performance reports, gifts and exchanges,
  desiderata files, and much more in a state-of-the-art package.

CARL Corporation
3800 East Florida Avenue, Suite 300
Denver, CO 80210
Website: www.carl.org
Aimed at the largest public, school, and regional library systems and
  library consortia, CARL's graphical user interfaces (GUIs), part
  of the CARL Information Management and Delivery System

(IMDS), provide a new graphical interface for Windows 95 and Windows NT. This streamlines the entire acquisitions process and eliminates unnecessary steps in ordering, receiving, and claiming of materials—all in a sleek, user-friendly format that will be a joy to those who are Windows oriented.

Data Research Associates, Inc. (DRA)
1276 N. Warson Road
St. Louis, MO 63132
Website: www.dra.com
One of the oldest systems vendors in the business, DRA has developed a new system, TAOS, which combines a complete Windows-based automation system into one package that is also a World Wide Web tool for all the library's OPAC needs: circulation, cataloging, acquisitions, and serials modules, plus an ILL module. All modules have multilingual capabilities, even in non-Roman character sets such as Chinese, Japanese, and Korean. The acquisitions module provides all the functions one might expect in a sophisticated system, including optional EDI capability.

epixtech (formerly Ameritech Library Services)
400 Dynix Drive
Provo, UT 84604
Website: www.amlibs.com
Ameritech, now epixtech, has refined its best-selling Dynix and Horizon automated library systems to meet the needs of today's more complex library operations in a Windows NT or UNIX environment. The full range of automated acquisitions functions is available and can support a variety of Web browsers running on PCs, Macs, or network computers, and provides for enriched BISAC and electronic ordering as well as EDIfact ordering and invoicing.

ExLibris
1653 North Wells Street
Chicago, IL 60614–6001
Website: www.exlibris-usa.com
ExLibris's Aleph 500 is a fully integrated system that is designed to serve as the core of the next-generation digital library. Its modules include Web and GUI PAC, circulation, cataloging, serials control, acquisitions, and ILL. The acquisitions module provides ordering and receiving, vendor information and control, and fund accounting, with advanced functions for the pooling of orders from various departments and budget fund sources. It also provides vendor communications via standard means or such elec-

tronic protocols as EDI, and converts foreign currencies to the Euro as well as to the local currency.

Gaylord Information Systems
P.O. Box 4901
Syracuse, NY 13221–4901
Website: www.gaylord.com/automation
Gaylord's Polaris Integrated Library system is a nonmodular, completely integrated, native Windows NT system, offering complete access to integrated cataloging, serials, acquisitions, circulation, and system administration, and provides a Web-based, public-access client and Windows-based, technical-services client. The latter enables the acquisitions librarian to easily maintain supplier profiles, search local and external sources for Web records, and create firm orders, subscriptions, standing orders, blanket orders, and rental plans. Orders can be placed using paper forms or computer-to-computer electronic transfers (FTP, BISAC, and EDI), and staff can link orders to funds and track encumbrances and expenditures, all based on Microsoft components to reduce costs for the system and increase reliability.

Geac
9 Technology Drive
P.O. Box 5150
Westborough, MA 01581–5150
Website: www.library.geac.com
Geac's ADVANCE and PLUS are comprehensive UNIX-system-based solutions whose integrated client/server and Web-based applications provide the newest technology available to manage workflow, and sophisticated but user-friendly access to information sources worldwide. Its modules include PAC, circulation, cataloging and authority control, acquisitions, serials control, and a management reporting system for any size library or library system; they support such industry standards for acquisitions as BISAC and X12. Perhaps best of all, it provides an evolutionary approach that allows customers to continue to add or use some of the newer technologies without scrapping the whole system and starting all over when they are ready to upgrade, as is the case with most other systems.

Innovative Interfaces (III)
5850 Shellmound Way
Emeryville, CA 94608
Website: www.iii.com
III has long been a leader in the industry with its Innopaq system, but its new Millennium modules are designed to build on the older system and at the same time employ the newest technology. Millennium is a Web-based system that offers a broad range of functionality in circulation, acquisitions, serials control, cataloging, authority control, management reporting, ILL, and other areas. The acquisitions module is fully integrated with the rest of the system and performs all functions associated with acquisition of all types of library materials via purchase, gift, exchange, and so on. It provides a full fund-accounting system and the ability to handle all types of transactions. Various electronic interfaces for sending orders and claims to all major vendors as well as receiving invoices and approval-plan data from them are available, as is the capability to automatically create item records from order records as items are received.

The Library Corporation
Research Park
Inwood, WV 25428–9733
Website: www.tlcdelivers.com
TLC's newest system, Library.Solution, is a turnkey, fully integrated automation system using Windows NT software that runs on PC-compatible computers in a user-friendly graphical interface environment catering to smaller and medium-sized libraries, although it is not limited to same. Its Library.Acquire subsystem is designed to manage the entire acquisitions process including purchasing, invoice management, fund accounting, and all other aspects of the process, including EDI; like the parent system, it is designed to grow and to support future enhancements and developments in automated acquisitions.

SIRS Mandarin, Inc.
P.O. Box 2348
Boca Raton, FL 33427–2348
Website: www.sirs.com
SIRS Mandarin M3 is a brand new system built on the older Mandarin, and is designed as an expandable turnkey hardware system that will be provided free of charge to existing Mandarin customers in good standing. The system is intended for school and smaller libraries that want a sophisticated system but don't have the funds for a large, integrated system. M3's Z39.50 model gives

the library the ability to share its catalog and resources via the Web. The acquisitions module is an integrated purchasing application that allows the librarian to create purchase orders in a single window, track orders, generate claims, perform fund accounting, and print reports on just about any acquisitions processes—all at a very reasonable cost.

Sirsi Corporation
689 Discovery Drive
Huntsville, AL 35806
Website: www.sirsi.com
Sirsi's UnicornOASIS is a full-function, library-management system designed exclusively for public libraries. Its simple, easy-to-use interface allows the librarian to utilize all the sophisticated features of a large-scale automation system at a small-scale cost. This interface, WorkFlows, uses icons and wizards to perform a variety of tasks and allows the user to be automatically prompted with the correct screen when necessary. The WorkFlows' interface functions include circulation, cataloging and authority control, inventory, serials control, and acquisitions, in a system that is user friendly and intuitive while still fulfilling sophisticated system requirements.

VTLS Inc.
1701 Kraft Drive
Blacksburg, VA 24060
Website: www.vtls.com
VTLS's Virtua is a Windows-based, client-server, integrated, library-automation system designed specifically to handle multimedia applications in a distributed network environment. Its acquisitions subsystem uses tabs, floating menus, and additional access points to allow quick navigation through the database, with the further benefit of being able to adapt to various and disparate libraries' priorities, policies, and procedures. All the acquisitions functions needed in a sophisticated program using the latest technology are included: vendor records (with a specific default vendor capability and default due dates), purchase-order production, varying order types (standard orders, approval plans, blanket orders, and gift items), fund accounting, claims and invoice processing and payment, currency adjustment, receipt reporting status, online searching of databases and downloading of cataloging records, and holding records—all simple and easy to use because of the graphical user interface and smooth workflow processes.

GLOSSARY

acquisitions. All the procedures involved in obtaining materials for libraries, from processing orders through check-in of materials received. May or may not include selection and fund accounting; may or may not include materials obtained through gifts or exchanges.

advance. Monies paid to the author before publication against future royalty earnings.

approval plan. Agreement between library and vendor (usually a wholesaler) that calls for vendor to supply one copy of each book either published or distributed by the vendor; subject to certain restrictions imposed by the library, such as subject, format, or price. Books are usually returnable for credit if not wanted.

back order. Refers to material ordered but not shipped at the time of the order.

backlist title. Title in a publisher's output whose sales are consistent enough over a period of time to justify the publisher's keeping it in print.

bibliographic data. All the pertinent information that defines a specific book, including author, title, edition or volume, publisher, publication date, and ISBN.

bid. Situation whereby a library solicits from all available vendors and offers all or most of its business to the vendor that offers the highest discounts.

billing price (or *billed price*). The cost of the book after it has been discounted or has had a surcharge added to the price; the invoice price.

binding. Method by which the pages of a book are held together; a book's cover.

blanket-order plan. Similar to *approval plan*, although vendor is usually the publisher; books are not returnable if not wanted. Vendor supplies one copy of each title published or each title in certain subject area, such as juvenile books, fiction, and so on.

blockbuster complex. The tendency on the part of some publishers to sign authors—such as John Grisham, Stephen King, Danielle Steel—whose books are virtually guaranteed to sell in large quantities over a very brief time span.

boards. The various kinds of stiffened paperboard used for a book's cover.

book club. A subscriber service that supplies books through the mail; examples include Book-of-the-Month Club, Literary Guild, Quality Paperback Book Club.

book designer. Person responsible for how a book looks; designs cover and page layout.

book distribution. Defined by the Book Industry Study Group as including book ordering; order processing; reordering; physical movement of books; inventory control; returns processing; receivables, credit, and collections; and data-processing support for all these functions.

Book Industry Study Group (BISG). A group from the Association of American Publishers (AAP) that performs occasional surveys of trends or problems in the book-distribution industry.

book promotion. What a publisher does to drum up interest in a title; may include author tours, autographing sessions, television appearances, and the like.

cancellation period. The period of time a library allows a vendor to provide a book before canceling an order; ninety days is a common cancellation period.

chain bookstore. Bookstore that is part of a group run by a single owner, such as Borders or Barnes & Noble.

claim. Notice sent to vendor asking why an ordered book has not been provided.

collection development. The process by which librarians examine their collections for strengths and weaknesses; attempts to correct weaknesses by carefully selecting and purchasing in those areas and weeding materials that have outlived their usefulness.

discount. Percentage deducted from the list or cover price of a book. Discounts may differ sharply from vendor to vendor.

drop ship. Mechanism whereby library orders books from vendor, vendor orders from producer, producer ships products to library, producer bills vendor, vendor bills library. It is as silly as it sounds and should be avoided by library book purchasers at all cost.

EOM (end of the month) discount. An incentive offered by vendors to get customers to pay bills early; usually 1 or 2 percent additional discount may be deducted by the customer if bill is paid by the end of the month.

electronic ordering. Using a computer, a modem, and certain software, the customer transmits order via a dedicated telephone line directly into the vendor's database. Order may also be transmitted via the Internet. Also known as *online ordering.*

encumber. To set aside or commit money to pay for materials ordered; moneys can only be unencumbered when materials are paid for or when orders not received are canceled.

fill rate. The percentage of materials ordered that is actually supplied by a vendor over a given period of time.

foreign book. Book published outside the United States. Certain vendors specialize in library orders for foreign books from certain countries or groups of countries.

freight pass through (FPT). Mechanism designed by publishers for retail booksellers; price charged to bookseller (or library) is usually fifty cents less than book cover price indicates, to cover shipping costs for bookseller/library.

frontlist title. Part of the publisher's current season's output; receives substantial publicity in order to promote sales.

fund accounting. In terms of book acquisitions, the process whereby departmental or branch accounts within the library are charged for what they have purchased.

galleys. Photocopies of a book's pages, before final corrections are made. Often glued together (bound galley) and sent to reviewers so book can be reviewed in advance of publication date.

gathering plan. Any formal plan or agreement with a vendor to receive materials automatically; see *standing-order plan, approval plan, blanket-order plan, Greenaway plan.*

genre book. Book written for specific group of readers; such as mystery, science fiction, fantasy, romance.

government publication. Monograph or serial published by a government agency, either national, state, or local.

Greenaway Plan. Plan devised by Emerson Greenaway of the Free Library of Philadelphia whereby a publisher provides one copy of every new title published (or within certain specified categories), usually at a very high discount; unwanted books are not returnable.

in print. Books still available from the publisher; not yet declared out of print.

independent distributor (ID). Vendor who distributes magazines, newspapers, and paperback books to retailers within a given territory.

International Standard Book Number. See *ISBN.*

International Standard Serial Number. See *ISSN.*

invoice. The vendor's formal bill for materials supplied.

invoice symbol. In the book trade, information supplied by vendor to explain why materials were not shipped; for example, NYP—not yet published; OP—out of print; OS—out of stock; NOP—not our publication.

ISBN (International Standard Book Number). A unique, ten-digit number assigned to every title, edition, and format published in most countries of the world. Essential for precise identification in searching and online ordering.

ISSN (International Standard Serial Number). Unique, eight-digit number assigned to each serial published in most countries of the world.

jobber. One who purchases materials from producers for resale to others. Book jobbers purchase books for resale to libraries, bookstores, and others. Often used interchangeably with "wholesaler" in the book trade.

lease plan. Agreement with a vendor (usually a wholesaler) to rent books in high demand and either return them when demand has lessened or purchase them at nominal price.

library binding. Sturdy, hardcover binding in which pages are stitched together before being glued into the book cover. Used primarily for children's books because of heavy wear and tear. Usually more expensive than trade binding.

library edition. See *library binding*.

list. A publisher's entire inventory of books still in print. May also refer to projected inventory, for example, the 2000 fall list includes those books that will be published in the fall of 2000.

list price. The price that appears on the cover of the book; the publisher's suggested retail price. See also *freight pass through*.

McNaughton Plan. Book-leasing plan for libraries administered by Brodart Corporation.

manufacturing costs. Variable costs for producing the book, including paper, printing, and binding. Costs are variable because they depend on the number of copies that are eventually printed. Part of total production cost.

mark-up. Whatever percentage of price increase booksellers or wholesalers wish to add to their discounted price.

mass-market paperback. Paper-covered book of a size that will fit into common rack displays, usually $6\frac{3}{4}$ x $4\frac{1}{8}$. Originally distributed by periodical and newspaper distributors, but more recently book wholesalers are handling them as well.

merger. When one company puts together its assets with those of another through purchase or takeover.

midlist title. Book on that part of a publisher's list that does not receive major publicity or promotion.

monograph. A book that is complete in itself, that is, not a serial.

net price. The price charged for an item, less discount.

on approval. Books provided to libraries by vendors for examination in light of possible purchase.

online ordering. Using a computer and modem, the customer transmits orders via a dedicated telephone line directly into the vendor's database. Also known as *electronic ordering.*

out of print (OP). No longer available from the publisher.

out of stock (OS). Not available from publisher or wholesaler, but not yet declared out of print.

out of stock indefinitely (OSI). Quaint euphemism used by publishers to denote a title that for some reason they do not wish to declare out of print but are unlikely to ever reprint. One step away from *OP.*

outsourcing. Refers to a library handing one or more of its functions over to be performed by a vendor.

overhead. The fixed cost of running a business. All the general costs other than costs for materials and production: salaries and benefits, rent, office supplies, telephones, office equipment, and so on.

perfect binding. Binding that glues pages or signatures into the book's cover. Used for most paperback books, and increasingly for hardcovers.

plant cost. The fixed cost of producing a book includes composition, typesetting, design, color separations. It is a fixed cost because these things need to be done only once in the production process.

prebinding. Process of taking only the pages of a book from a publisher and binding them to Library Binding Institute standards; extremely sturdy, but the usual result is an unattractive and expensive book. Used primarily for children's titles.

press run. See *print run.*

print run. The number of copies ordered by the publisher for a printing. The initial print run is the number of books printed for the first edition; one or more additional print runs may be requested after the initial run.

production costs. All the costs of producing books: plant (fixed) costs and manufacturing (variable) costs.

publisher. Person or company that turns an author's work into a published book.

purchase order. The library's official order form for materials to be provided by the vendor.

quality paperback. Paper books that are larger in size than mass-market paperbacks and generally higher in price. Usually distributed by book wholesalers.

reinforced binding. Hardcover binding in which a few stitches are used to hold pages together before they are glued into cover; stronger than trade binding but much weaker than true library binding.

religious publishing. Books published by religious denominations or societies or by companies that specialize in publishing books relating to a certain religion; includes the Jewish Publication Society, Paulist Press, Augsburg Fortress Press.

remainder dealer. One who specializes in buying publishers' overstock and then reselling to retailers and libraries at bargain prices.

remainders. Unsold copies of a book that the publisher chooses to sell to a *remainder dealer*; once remainders are thus sold, books are considered out of print.

reprint. A new printing of a book.

returns. Books returned to the publisher for full or partial credit within a certain time period; a huge problem for the publishing industry.

royalties. Monies paid to authors based on sales of their books; a percentage of the revenues.

selection. The process of choosing which titles should go into a library's collection.

serial. Publication issued in successive parts for an indefinite period.

May be a magazine, annual, newspaper, proceedings, or numbered monograph in a series.

short discount. Discount that is less than the standard trade discount. See also *trade discount.*

single binding. See *reinforced binding.*

small press publishing. Publishing by nontraditional publishers other than trade, university press, religious publishers. Often referred to as alternative or independent publishing.

standing-order plan. Gathering plan wherein the library is supplied with everything the publisher puts out except for stipulated exceptions. Also may refer to agreement to supply units in a series as they appear.

subsidy publishing. See *vanity publishing.*

takeover. Acquisition of one company by another; may be friendly or "hostile."

technical services. That group of library processes that handles the acquisitions, cataloging, and processing of materials selected.

trade binding. The binding of a trade book as it is issued from its publisher; usually hardcover.

trade book. Book intended for the general reader and sold to wholesalers, retail booksellers, and libraries.

trade discount. The usual discount on trade books; most likely higher than discounts on most other categories of books.

trade paperback. See *quality paperback.*

trade publisher. One who produces trade books.

turnkey system. Computer system that is offered for sale or lease; may consist of software only, or software and hardware.

university press publishing. Books published under the aegis of a university. Usually intended for the scholarly community, although recent trends indicate that more university presses are publishing books for the general reader.

vanity publishing. Books published under an arrangement whereby the author pays all costs; can be extremely costly, and books may be of inferior quality.

vendor. One who sells materials to a library; may be a publisher, wholesaler/jobber, or retailer.

wholesaler. Vendor who buys books from publishers for resale to libraries and bookstores; often used interchangeably with *jobber.*

young adult book. Book published by the children's or juvenile department of a trade publisher; intended for readers twelve to eighteen years old.

SELECTED ANNOTATED BIBLIOGRAPHY

BOOKS AND ARTICLES

American Library Association. 1984. *Guidelines for Handling Library Orders for In-print Monographic Publications*. 2d ed. Chicago: American Library Association. Short but complete overview of customary book-ordering procedures. A little outdated.

Benson, Allen C. 1997. *The Neal-Schuman Complete Internet Companion for Librarians*. 2d ed. New York: Neal-Schuman. Basic guide for those librarians who need a little help using the Net.

Bischoff, Liz, and Carol Chamberlain, eds. 1997. *Coping with the Electronic Library: Strategies for Technical Services and Collection Development*. New York: Neal-Schuman. Good look at current issues and solutions

Blumenthal, Joseph. 1997. *The Printed Book in America*. Boston: David R. Godine. As much a history of book printing as of the book itself; also informative about the history of publishing.

Bonn, Thomas L. 1982. *Undercover: An Illustrated History of American Mass Market Paperbacks*. New York: Penguin. Lively history with emphasis on cover art, which is so vital to the success of paperbacks.

Boss, Richard W. 1997. "Options for Acquisitions and Serials Control Automation in Libraries." *Library Technology Reports* (July–August).

Boswell, John. 1986. *The Awful Truth about Publishing: Why They Always Reject Your Manuscript . . . and What You Can Do about It*. New York: Warner. Agent/author gives a lot of solid information about trade publishing over the last few decades.

Brownmiller, Susan. 1983. "A Word from You—Confessions of an Ex-Blurb Writer." *New York Times Book Review* (January 12), 3.

Carter, Robert A. 1987. *Opportunities in Book Publishing Careers*. Lincolnwood, Ill.: NTC/Contemporary Publishing Group. A career guide that gives a fine overview of the entire publishing process.

Cohn, John, Anne L. Kelsey, and Keith Michael Fiels. 1997. *Planning for Automation*, 2d ed. New York: Neal-Schuman. Handy guide to working out all the steps and procedures for successful automation.

Coser, Lewis A., Charles Kadushin, and Walter W. Powell. 1983. *Books: The Culture and Commerce of Publishing*. New York: Basic Books. Informative and thought-provoking discussion of the influence of the book on American culture.

Crider, Allen Billy, ed. 1992. *Mass Market Paperback Publishing in America*. New York: Macmillan. A house-by-house history of the business, even those houses which are long gone.

Curley, Arthur, and Dorothy Broderick. 1985. *Building Library Collections*. 6th ed. Metuchen, N.J.: Scarecrow. In addition to two excellent chapters on "The Publishing Trade" and "Acquisitions," this book contains an introductory chapter, "Why Libraries Exist," that ought to be must reading at least once each year for anyone in acquisitions.

Curley, Marie T. 1968. *The Buckram Syndrome: A Critical Essay on Paperbacks in Public Libraries of the United States*. Chicago: American Library Association. More than thirty years old, but contains still-valid information about library elitism regarding paperback books.

Curtis, Richard. 1989. *Beyond the Bestseller: A Literary Agent Takes You Inside the Book Business*. New York: New American Library. You'll learn more about the real world of book publishing from this outspoken writer/agent/publisher than you will from reading all the textbooks in the world. A must for anyone really interested in the lowdown.

———. 1996. *Mastering the Business of Writing: A Leading Literary Agent Reveals the Secrets of Success*. New York: Allworth. Curtis is a pro when it comes to publishing. This is a highly useful guide to the economics (the "business") of the book industry, easy to read and fascinating in its insights.

Davis, Kenneth C. 1984. *Two-Bit Culture: The Paperbacking of America*. Boston: Houghton Mifflin. Another interesting history of the paperback. This one goes into how paperbacks have influenced American culture and vice versa.

Deitch, Joseph. 1982. "Moving Books Around." *Publishers Weekly* (December 17).

Dessauer, John P. 1993. *Book Publishing: What It Is, What It Does*. 2d ed. New York: Continuum. Good introduction to the industry except when Dessauer's antilibrary biases show through.

Eaglen, Audrey, 1984. "Chain Bookstores and Library Collection Building." *Collection Building* 6, no. 1 (spring).

Ensor, Pat, ed. 1997. *The Cybrarian's Manual*. Chicago: American Library Association. Dozens of articles by practitioners on everything you want or need to know about the automated library.

Evans, G. Edward. 2000. *Developing Library and Information Center Collections.* Littleton, Colo.: Libraries Unlimited. Good section on the entire acquisitions process in a newly updated edition of a basic reference tool.

Feldman, Gayle. 1988. "University Presses: A Changing Role." *Publishers Weekly* (September 23).

Flood, Susan, ed. 1998. *Guide to Managing Approval Plans.* Chicago: American Library Association. For those of you out there who just have to use approval plans, some good advice.

Ford, Stephen. 1973. *The Acquisition of Library Materials.* Chicago: American Library Association. The best guide ever written on how *not* to operate an acquisitions department. Not a single nit is unpicked.

Futas, Elizabeth. 1994. *Library Acquisition Policies and Procedures.* 2d ed. Phoenix, Ariz.: Oryx Press. A lot more policies than procedures, but a useful guide nevertheless.

Gardner, Richard K. 1981. *Library Collections: Their Origin, Selection, and Development.* New York: McGraw-Hill. Part 1 of this book is an excellent overview of the entire publishing process.

Geiser, Elizabeth, ed. 1985. *The Business of Book Publishing: Papers by Practitioners.* Phoenix, Ariz.: Westview. Solid information on the industry by a host of people who are (or, in some cases, were) involved in it. Not as current as it might be, but still of value.

Gorman, Michael, ed. 1998. *Technical Services Today and Tomorrow.* 2d ed. Littleton, Colo.: Libraries Unlimited. Few people know more about technical services than Gorman, and this collection of articles reflects his expertise in choosing what librarians need to know.

Greenfield, Howard. 1988. *Books: From Writer to Reader.* 2d ed. New York: Crown. Written for younger readers, this is still a very valuable overview of the business of book publishing and production.

Healey, Lisa, ed. 1994. *My First Year in Book Publishing: Real World Stories from America's Book Publishing Professionals.* New York: Walker. Contemporary workers of every sort and at every level in book publishing tell what their work is really like—even an indexer has his say!

Hilts, Paul, and James Lichtenberg. 1998. "Redefining Distribution." *Publishers Weekly* (December 21).

Hirshon, Arnold, and Barbara Winters. 1996. *Outsourcing Library Technical Services.* New York: Neal-Schuman. Written before the great 1996 Baker & Taylor brouhaha, but a good overview of the issues.

Imhoff, Kathleen R. 1996. *Making the Most of New Technology.* New York: Neal-Schuman. A nice introduction to some basic information about many aspects of the new technology and how to use it.

Katz, William A. 1980. *Collection Development: The Selection of Materials for Libraries.* New York: Holt, Rinehart and Winston. Contains an excellent chapter on "Ordering Books."

Kershner, Lois M. 1988. *Forms for Automated Library Systems: An Illustrated Guide for Selection, Design, and Use.* New York: Neal-Schuman. Not exactly new, but still an excellent source book, loaded with ideas and samples to use.

Kovacs, Diane. 2000. *Building Electronic Library Collections: The Essential Guide to Selection Criteria and Core Subject Collections.* New York: Neal-Schuman. Since indications are that library collections will become increasingly Web-based in the near future, this basic guide to all aspects of building electronic libraries not only will be of interest to selectors but also should prove valuable to the acquisitions staff who will also have to deal with the issue.

LaGuardia, Cheryl, and Barbara A. Mitchell. 1998. *Finding Common Ground: Creating the Library of the Future without Diminishing the Library of the Past.* New York: Neal-Schuman. Just what the title promises; the best of the old *can* be melded with the new.

Lovecy, Ian. 1984. *Automating Library Procedures: A Survivor's Handbook.* Phoenix, Ariz.: Oryx Press, 1984. Don't expect to use much of the information in this, but just be amused by what often is a very funny book.

Madison, Charles A. 1966. *Book Publishing in America.* New York: McGraw-Hill. A good one-volume history, readable and often fascinating.

Maryles, Daisy. 2000. "Connecting the Numbers." *Publishers Weekly* (January 10).

Meghabghab, Dania B. 1997. *Automating Media Centers and Small Libraries: A Microcomputer-based Approach.* Littleton, Colo.: Libraries Unlimited. Smaller libraries will find the information in this book helpful in using inexpensive personal computers to automate many procedures.

Melcher, Daniel. 1971. *Melcher on Acquisition.* Chicago: American Library Association. The best book on acquisitions ever written, but not too well accepted by librarians simply because Melcher (1) was not a librarian and (2) makes sense. A book ahead of its time.

Miller, Heather S. 1992. *Managing Acquisitions and Vendor Relations.* New York: Neal-Schuman. There's lots of good information here, but probably more than the nonspecialist cares to know; primarily for academic librarians.

Murray, Laura K. 1998. *Basic Internet for Busy Librarians: A Quick*

Course for Catching Up. Chicago: American Library Association. Everything you always wanted to know but didn't know whom to ask.

Pastine, Maureen, ed. 1997. *Collection Development: Access in the Virtual Library.* Binghamton, NY: Haworth. Good readings on issues facing libraries of the twenty-first century.

Pitkin, Gary M. 1996. *The National Electronic Library: A Guide to the Future for Library Managers.* Westport, Conn.: Greenwood. Thought-provoking readings for those who are trying to guide the destinies of twenty-first century libraries.

Potter, Clarkson N. 1990. *Who Does What and Why in Publishing: Writers, Editors, and Money Men.* New York: Birch Lane Press/ Carol Publishing Group. Clarkson Potter has been a publisher all his life, and it shows. An excellent, basic guide to the book-publishing business and its practitioners.

Raatma, Lucia. 1998. *How Books Are Made.* New York: Children's Press. A children's book, but an excellent, well-illustrated guide to all that goes into making a book.

Ross, Tom and Marilyn. 1994. *The Complete Guide to Self-Publishing.* 3d ed. Cincinnati: Writers Digest Books. There's lots here to be learned about every aspect of the writing, publishing, and promotion of books, even if you aren't a self-publisher.

Saunders, Laverna M., ed. 1999. *The Evolving Virtual Library: Visions and Case Studies.* Medford, N.J.: Information Today, Inc. A good look at the potential impact of technology on today's libraries, with a particularly informative, speculative article by Bernard A. Margolis, "A Paradox for the Public Library."

Schmidt, Karen A., ed. 1998. *Understanding the Business of Library Acquisitions.* 2d ed. Chicago: American Library Association. Good overview for the most part, although slanted toward academic libraries. The final section on "Methods of Accounting and Business Practices" is must reading for *anyone* in acquisitions, however.

Schneider, Karen G. 1999. "Let Your Fingers Do the Collection Development—Online." *American Libraries* (May).

Schreuders, Piet. 1981. *Paperbacks, U.S.A.: A Graphic History, 1939–1959.* San Diego: Blue Dolphin Enterprises. Another fine history of the paperback in its earlier heyday, emphasizing graphic elements.

Sellen, Betty-Carol, and Arthur Curley, eds. 1992. *The Collection Building Reader.* New York: Neal-Schuman. Collection of some of the best articles from this important journal, many having to do with the book-publishing industry.

Shatzkin, Leonard. 1982. *In Cold Type: Overcoming the Book Crisis.* Boston: Houghton Mifflin. Shatzkin has his own ideas about the publishing industry, and many of them are on target; provocative.

Smith, Ronald Ted. 1996. *Book Publishing Encyclopedia: The Secrets of Successful Publishing*. 2d ed. Sarasota, Fla.: Bookworld. Excellent guide to the business of publishing, especially on returns, distribution, pricing.

Stewart, Barbara. 1997. *Neal-Schuman Directory of Library Technical Services Home Pages*. New York: Neal-Schuman. There's a lot of information out there in other libraries' home pages, from lists of the best publisher and vendor home pages to library acquisitions departments home pages, and more.

Swan, James. 1996. *Automating Small Libraries*. Fort Atkinson, Wisc.: Highsmith. The very best, step-by-step guide to the things you need to know in automating library procedures and processes. Must reading for anyone considering switching from manual to modern.

Tebbel, John. *A History of Book Publishing in the United States*. 4 vols. New York: R. R. Bowker, various copyrights. For the truly dedicated; however, this massive history will reward the real book buffs among you.

———. 1987. *Between Covers: The Rise and Transformation of American Book Publishing*. New York: Oxford University Press. Good short history of the industry.

Walker, Barbara J. 1998. *Developing Christian Fiction Collections for Children and Adults: Selection Criteria and a Core Collection*. New York: Neal-Schuman. As mentioned in the text of this book, libraries are now serving their Christian clientele, and this volume will help them a great deal.

Whiteside, Thomas. 1981. *The Blockbuster Complex*. New York: Columbia University Press. Not brand new, but still sheds a lot of light on the whole phenomenon of blockbuster titles, and its effect on the business of publishing.

JOURNALS

American Bookseller. The official journal of the American Booksellers Association. Provides much information that other journals do not. Monthly.

Book Alert. Prepublication announcements of forthcoming future bestsellers, noteworthy midlist titles, children's books, university and independent press selections, and spoken word audios. Free. Monthly.

Book Research Quarterly. Often heavily academic, but still basic; for anyone who is serious about keeping up with the business of books. Quarterly.

B P Report. Chock full of information about book publishing; has news before you see it in *Publishers Weekly.* Necessary for any major acquisitions department. Weekly.

Collection Building. Contains frequent articles and columns on publisher/library relations and other issues in book distribution. Quarterly.

Computers in Libraries. Good coverage of recent developments in and new uses of computer technology in the library environment. Ten issues per year.

Feminist Bookstore News. Trade journal for the women-in-print movement, but highly useful for libraries; extensive reviews of both mainstream and small press titles of interest to women. Bimonthly.

Library Acquisitions: Practice and Theory. Often highly academic, but a valid tool for the acquisitions librarian nevertheless. Quarterly.

Library Hi-Tech. Takes a scholarly approach to computers and technology for libraries, but can occasionally shed some light on issues and trends. Quarterly.

Library Journal. Contains regular columns and frequent articles on automation in libraries. Twice monthly, except for single issues in July, August, and December.

Publishers Weekly. This is the one tool the acquisitions department must have; the bible of the publishing industry. Weekly.

School Library Journal. Has excellent columns and many articles on various aspects of automation and libraries. Monthly.

Small Press Book Review. Book reviews for online users; can be downloaded free by e-mail at *henryberry@aol.com.*

TOOLS OF THE TRADE

ABA Bookbuyers Handbook. Official online publication of the American Booksellers Association. Profiles thousands of American publishers regarding their business terms, discounts, and more. A vital tool for major acquisitions departments. Annual.

ABA Newswire. Weekly report on publishing news, particularly about author tours.

Books in Print. The print version is out of date the day you get it, but nonetheless an important tool for libraries. If at all possible, get the online version, which is updated frequently. Annual (print edition).

The Bowker Annual. Basic statistics and trends in both book publishing and libraries. Annual.

Forthcoming Books in Print. Lists bibliographic data on books months in advance of publication date. Bimonthly.

Literary Market Place. Just about anything you need to know about publishing, distribution, services. Annual.

Publishers, Distributors & Wholesalers of the United States. Extensive information not so easily found elsewhere; covers some 95,000 active U.S. publishers, distributors, associations, and wholesalers, including many independent and small publishers. Contains ordering information, e-mail and Website addresses, discount schedules, and returns policies. Annual.

Publishers Trade List Annual. A lot of publishers' catalogs bound together in six volumes. Since it's out of date the day you get it, not very useful except for retrospective buying.

Small Press Record of Books in Print. CD-ROM only. Makes it easy to find information on some 45,000 small press titles from more than 5,000 presses. Updated frequently.

Subject Guide to Books in Print. A subject locator for titles listed in *Books in Print.* Better for collection development than acquisitions as a rule. Annual.

Words on Cassette. The *"Books in Print"* of spoken word cassettes; a comprehensive listing. Annual.

INDEX

ABOUT THE AUTHOR

Audrey Eaglen retired recently after 25 years as Acquisitions Librarian for the Cuyahoga County Public Library System in Cleveland, Ohio. During her career she was active at many levels in the American Library Association. She was a frequent contributor to a number of professional journals and edited several herself. She also served as a speaker and facilitator at workshops and conferences on library acquisitions all over the United States and Canada, and taught courses at the Kent State University Graduate School of Library and Information Science. At this time, she acts as a professional book reviewer and tends her garden.